SURVIVING
the HOME INSPECTION

by Paul Duffau

CruiserPublications

This book is licensed for your personal enjoyment and use. Information contained in this work has been obtained by Cruiser Publications, LLC from sources believed to be reliable.

However, neither Cruiser Publications, LLC nor the author guarantee the completeness or accuracy of the information presented. Neither Cruiser Publications, LLC nor the author are shall be held responsible for errors, omissions, or damages arising from your or another's use of the information in this work.

This work is published with the understanding the publisher nor the author are providing information, and that individuals acting on such information are responsible for any events that may occur.

Neither the publisher nor the author are rendering any engineering services or other licensed professional services. Should such services be desired or required, we recommend retaining the services of the appropriate professionals.

The Essential Seller's Guide for SURVIVING the Home Inspection

Copyright © 2015 Paul Duffau

This book, or parts thereof, may not be reproduced in any form without written permission.

Published 2015 by Cruiser Publications
www.cruiserpublications.com

Cover art from Dreamstime
Book design copyright © 2015

Cruiser Publications
ISBN 978-0-9889479-5-5

All rights reserved.

Table of Contents

Introduction	1
Chapter 1—Hiring Your Own Inspector	6
Chapter 2—Utilities	12
Chapter 3—Curb Appeal	17
Chapter 4 – Exteriors	23
Chapter 5 – Interiors	29
Chapter 6 - Plumbing	45
Chapter 7 – Heating and Cooling	50
Chapter 8 – Crawlspaces	56
Chapter 9 – The Attic	60
Chapter 10 – Environmental Conditions	66
Chapter 11 – The Inspection is Imminent	73

Introduction

"Hi, my name is Paul and I'm the home inspector your Realtor warned you about. How are you?"

It's a silly question isn't it, that last "How are you?" You're stressed. A stranger is about to enter your house with the sole purpose of inspecting your home from top to bottom. Is he going to nitpick your home to death? Will he treat your home and your privacy with the respect they deserve? Most importantly, will this guy on your front porch kill your deal?

I understand this stress. I sold a house and moved in 2007. After having lived there for three years and performing my own home inspection, I knew that house inside and out. The buyers wanted their own inspection and I agreed. Even though I knew that house better than anyone on the planet and I also knew I was a better inspector than the one the buyers retained, I was stressed.

When I introduce myself to a seller during a home inspection, I know two things. One, that you are pleased because you have an offer on your home (Yea!); and, two, that you are stressed to meet me. You know that I am going to be spending three or four hours in your house – your HOME – and the perception of my job is to nit-pick it to death. Which isn't really my job, by the way, but we're talking about perceptions here – yours and the buyers. I try to set the seller at ease. I explain my job, tell you that my goal is to perform my inspection and leave your home without a trace that I was ever there.

The introduction for the buyers is a bit different since I've already talked to them on the phone. We've already had a discussion on what I'll be looking at and what for, whether I'll be up on the roof or in the crawlspace, how I mark up my reports. *They* want me to nit-pick the house, to find things.

Because then they are going to ask you to either fix some things or give them even more money back.

The home sales arena was actually much worse than what was being reported on the news throughout the decline. In December of 2011, the National Association of Realtors admitted that the figures that they had supplied the media overstated home sales for the years 2007 to 2011 by double counting homes. The total error was about 15 percent according to CoreLogic, an independent data firm that was among the first to question the disparity of the NAR's numbers.

As I write this, one in five buyers is an investor. Investors by their nature are not looking to give you a top price for your home. They are looking for deals for themselves that will provide cash flow and be profitable. Their behavior drives down prices – in every neighborhood – and affects your home sale by changing the "comps" used by appraisers to determine value.

There are other factors at work, too. The next generation of home buyers, young professionals, are saddled with tremendous student loan debt and face a jobs market that is reluctant to hire. This directly impacts the bottom end, or starter home, market and in turn limits move-up buyers.

Throughout 2014, prices rebounded nicely, but we again have warning signs on the horizon. Sub-prime mortgages have returned. Rising prices for commodities from corn to electricity, meat to healthcare, mean that a larger portion of income goes to basic living expenses and leaving less income for home purchases and repairs. Inflation is officially listed at 3.0 percent for 2011 – the last year that I have data. That inflation rate excludes energy and food prices from its calculation so the actual rate is higher than the official rate on the items that we all use. Personally, I'm addicted to food and I imagine Idaho in February can get quite nippy without a reliable and inexpensive supply of energy.

Skittish Buyers

Buyers are becoming increasingly cautious when they consider buying a home. "Individual sellers, real estate agents and builders are all feeling the effects of growing wariness on the part of prospective buyers," writes Glenn Fowler in the *The New York Times* in November of 2011. This is manifesting itself in several ways. First, the buyers are slower to make an offer and are looking at more homes before they do. With high resale inventories and deep discounts on new homes, the competition for an offer is at an all-time high. Buyers are aware of this and are making decisions accordingly.

Second, once they have made an offer, they are doing more due diligence. The expectation of selling a "money-pit" for a profit *a la* Flip This House

The Buyer

Traditionally in United States marketplace, it is the homebuyer who purchases the services of the home inspector. The buyers will purchase this inspection to get two things. The first is peace of mind that they aren't buying a money pit. Today's homebuyers are far less likely to have the background or handyman skills that our grandfather's generation had and this has led to the growth of the inspection industry. Once upon a time, the buyer might have been a carpenter or an electrician or had worked with his Dad or Uncle doing those types of jobs. They would have had some experience and, more importantly, perspective about homes.

Today's generation has interned at a white-collar jobs while going to college and then entered the professional or retail world instead of a trade. Consequently, they know far less about housing than previous homeowners and need more advice. They need a home inspector to fill that need.

The second reason is that the inspection is often used to control the price of the home purchase. With the go-go market from 1999 to 2007, homes were getting multiple offers, often escalating as they came in as buyers tried to one-up the competition and get into a new home. And while buyers were getting inspections, they often had very limited negotiation room because of those back up offers. It was a make-or-break proposition for them. If the home was in reasonably good shape, they completed the transaction. If it wasn't, they walked. Asking for money or repairs often led the seller – you – to say "No Thanks!" and move on to the next offer.

The other psychological factor that worked in the sellers favor then was the pervasive thought that real estate always goes up, so the buyer could purchase a fixer and, doing little or no repairs, sell it for a profit in five years.

That was then....

Times have changed. Since the top of the housing bubble, home prices have declined about a third, taking with it much of your equity. To add insult to injury, you are competing against the very banks – Bank of America, Wells Fargo, Citi – who helped create the bubble and the resulting cratering of the housing industry. Plus, the foreclosure market continues to erode pricing for homes in certain markets. There is also the overhang of the "shadow inventory," those homes that have been foreclosed but not put on the market yet which is driving up the supply and not counted in the official figures.

disappeared in 2006. They are planning on living in the home longer and they expect it to be in better condition. Since they can no longer count on housing appreciation to cover poor decisions or pay for repairs, they want cleaner, better maintained homes – or, if they can't get that, total fixers at a very steep discount. Ideally, they want your cleaner, better maintained home at a very steep discount.

The banks are not your friend in the process. They have become reluctant to lend money to anybody other than a perfect client with surplus cash and an excellent credit rating. This over-reaction to the sub-prime debacle is limiting the numbers of qualified buyers that you have access to and allows the ones that can get financing greater control in dictating terms. The buyers that do qualify are usually looking to limit any more out-of-pocket expenses. They want turnkey homes at bargain basement prices.

And since they plan on living in these homes longer, they are looking at the long-term operating costs and health issues that may be present. Remember the increases in energy costs? They want to know what the average utilities will be. If they are too high, buyers will want to know why and they will ask their inspector to find out for them (disregard for the moment that this isn't in the scope of an inspection).

Your goal is to give them what they want – but at a price you want and can afford. To do that, you need to take on...

The Buyer's Gunslinger

Yes, it's melodramatic but that's how the buyer too often looks at me, the home inspector. They *want* me to find problems (some will insist that a particular component must be marked defective even if I don't agree. More than once, I've offered to return their money).

Each item in the report is negotiable and good Realtors® will guide the buyers on what is reasonable and ordinary. Unless the home is new or nearly new, the house will have some varying degrees of wear and tear. The better Realtors provide guidance to their clients on this and will help them to focus on the big items, not the ding in the door. Even so, some buyers will demand everything be fixed. I had one buyer in early 2007 who told me bluntly, "Find everything. I don't want to have to do anything to this home for 20 years." It was a completely unrealistic expectation on his part but one that I see occurring more and more often.

Introduction

Some inspectors thrive in the hired gun role and view their job as finding anything they can to help the buyer win a better deal. This is fundamentally unfair to you, the seller. The inspector is supposed to be fair and impartial. I see it again and again that inspection reports are being wielded as a means of beating up the seller and gaining concessions. I advise all my clients that no house is perfect, not even a new one, and that we can expect to have at least a few items on the list of repairs.

There are actually three "lists" that I talk about: the "to-do" list of small repairs, the learn-to-live-with-it list of things that don't meet current standards (such as wall framing in a 1902 Victorian home), and, the "big, scary" items list. The last one frequently involves a major surprise for the seller – they often didn't know they had termites, for example – while the "to-do" list generates the most disagreement.

It is the "to-do" list that causes the most problems. And this is where this book will be invaluable. Disagreement occurs when you, the seller, and they, the buyer, think that the other guy should be responsible for a given repair. You can't control how the inspector records his findings and you really cannot control how his or her agent is going to advise the buyer and frame the negotiation. What you can control are many of the "to-do" items by removing them before the inspection.

So, let me re-introduce myself. I'm Paul, the home inspector who is going to help you turn the inspection contingency from a voyage into the unknown to an opportunity to impress the buyers and their inspector while improving your chances for selling your home. At the end of every chapter, I have provided checklists that you can use to make sure you're prepared.

Ready to start?

Chapter 1—Hiring Your Own Inspector

Should You Hire Your Own Inspector?

Oftentimes, first-time home sellers wonder if they should hire someone to perform an inspection prior to listing their home for sale. Unfortunately there is not an easy answer. If you ask a home inspector, the answer is likely to be an unequivocal "Yes!" If you ask your Realtor, the answer may be an equally emphatic "No!"

They are both right so let's look at the three primary reasons to hire a home inspector and a few reasons why you shouldn't. More importantly, let's find out which decision is right for you.

Reason #1 – Make Necessary Repairs

A home inspection is useful for building a "to-do" list that will help get the home ready for market. This type of inspection is very effective at identifying issues in the home that you can correct before you officially list your home on the market. This could range from an item as simple as replacing a smoke alarm battery to upgrading the insulation, or getting the sinks to drain properly.

You won't normally fix everything on the list, but most people anticipate putting at least a modest amount of effort into the repairs. Your goal is to present the home to the buyer in better than average condition, which will encourage more and better offers. As an added plus, you have the chance to use the repairs that you have already completed as part of the negotiation process, and limit the opportunity for the buyer's inspector or agent to over-inflate repair costs—which will drive the selling price down.

Another advantage is the opportunity to pick the inspector's brain on what is really a necessary repair versus those items that are usually ignored. Since he is working for you, his unbiased advice regarding repairs, the costs that might be associated with them, and the relative difficulty of making the repair is very valuable information. Use this new data to prioritize the most important items that must be addressed, the small items that are quick fixes, and the ones that you should disclose to the buyer, though not always fix. Remember that no home is perfect, so having some items left on the list is not unusual.

Reason #2 – Disclosure

A home inspection will protect yourself legally from disclosure-related types of issues. Every state has its own disclosure forms and requirements that you, as the seller, need to fill out. Mistakes on these forms can be terribly expensive if a buyer decides to take you to court. By bringing in the inspector, you have an impartial third party who can provide you with most of the information needed for your disclosures. Keep in mind that the inspector cannot provide *all* of this information. For example *Was there ever a flood?* may be a question that the inspector can't answer since the repairs were completed eight years ago and there are no visual clues.

Releasing the home inspection report as part of your disclosure will have the added benefit of showing goodwill. You will appear as an honest person who is candid in your presentation of the home and the buyer is much more likely to trust a person who is making every effort to be open and honest.

The disclosure issue cannot be minimized. It used to be very rare for me to get a call from new homeowners asking about failed inspections and seller disclosures. However, the disclosure issues are on the rise and I now receive a call every few months from homebuyers that want to know if they should sue their inspector, the agent, or the sellers. Some areas of the country are more prone to litigious behavior, such as California, Florida, Arizona, but even in the deeply rural area that I live in, the change is noticeable.

Reason #3 – Discourage the Buyer from Hiring an Inspector

Doing an inspection prior to listing your home may discourage the buyer from hiring his own home inspector. While many home inspectors advertise that a pre-listing inspection may encourage the buyer to forgo their own inspection, I don't wholly agree. Even when I perform an inspection for the seller, I always recommend that the buyer have his own inspection done.

That seems a bit contradictory so why do I suggest it?

Because you never want a perceived conflict of interest on your part or the inspector's part. Remember, we are trying to build trust throughout the process and limiting the choices of the buyer or even trying to influence them to self-limit can work to build doubt. It is, however, a successful strategy and I estimate that half or more of the homes I pre-inspect do not get inspected by a buyer's inspector.

What's the Downside to Hiring an Inspector?

According to a quick search on the Internet, there are no disadvantages for sellers who have used pre-listing inspections.

I disagree.

The prevailing thought is that you are laying off the risks of lawsuits and judgments to the home inspector, who surely carries Errors and Omissions insurance. There are two problems with this perspective: first, the assumption that the inspector is insured; and, second, that the aggrieved buyer will only name the inspector in any potential litigation.

The truth is that a third or more of the inspectors *do not* carry insurance. It is not required in most states and is expensive to hold, so many inspectors skip it. The other issue, involving litigation, is that lawyers tend to name everyone they can in a suit: the inspector, your agent, you, even your dog if the lawyer thinks they have any monetary value.

So, what are the risks?

The major risk is that the inspector finds a material defect such as with the termites I mentioned earlier or an electrical panel that is a shock and fire hazard that you were not previously aware of. Once you know you have a material defect in the property, you will be required to disclose it. This could range from an old water event to sub-par roofing materials or worse. This can substantially impact your sale price even if you repair the defect. Obviously, if the buyer discovers it with his own home inspection, it will have the same negative effect.

There is a second risk as well. Let's assume that you hired an inspector, he did his inspection, and gave you the report. You look it over and are relieved—there's not much to be fixed. You do the light repairs that were recommended and, when you get an offer, you confidently invite the buyer to get his own inspection. Then you get the buyer's inspection report back and the second inspector has found multiple problems with your "clean" home. What just happened?

Likely, one of two things—and, unfortunately, only one of which you can directly control. The first possibility, the one not fully under your control, is that the inspector for the buyer feels he needs to create issues to justify a fee.

The second is that you hired the wrong inspector.

How to Pick your Inspector

One of the best compliments I ever received came from a client who had used me on a small commercial project. The project was interesting—a turn-of-the-century storefront. A few years later he called me to inspect his home before he sold it. Why did he call me? He said that he wanted to take the best home inspector off the market, forcing the buyers to select a lesser inspector.

I am going to presume that you, like most people, do not have a home inspector on speed dial. If you decide that a pre-listing inspection makes sense for you, let's look at the factors that you will need to evaluate in order to hire the right inspector.

> *Experience.* You need to have an inspector that has the professional background—education, time in the field, previous occupations—to be as thorough as possible. You should expect no less than five years of inspector experience in your region. Previous experience in the building trades or as a code certified inspector is a plus.
>
> *Licensed.* Not every state has licensure but if yours does, your inspector must be licensed. If things get contentious, the more qualified your inspector, the more likely you are to come out clean from a sticky situation. Licensing is only an entry level requirement. Look for additional certifications from ASHI (American Society of Home Inspectors) or NAHI (National Association of Home Inspectors). Ask to see copies of his professional license as well as any applicable business licenses.
>
> *Reports.* You will need a detailed report, preferably in a narrative format, that will elaborate on the specific condition that needs correction. The inspector should also be willing to

do a follow-up inspection to document that repairs were made. Expect to pay extra for this service.

Insured. As I mentioned before, the inspector should be carrying Errors and Omissions (E&O) insurance as well as General Liability insurance. Ask to see copies of his insurance binders.

Fees

So I'm sure you're wondering at this point, *how much will all this cost?* While the fee is important, keep in mind that you are looking for a level of exceptional service. A typical home inspection is going to cost somewhere between $300 and $500 depending on your region, the size of your home, and the level of services involved. Each region will have different pricing structures with some charging extra for building elements such as crawlspaces or older homes. Be aware that the low cost bidder is likely one that lacks some of the primary credentials that you need.

Another element to look for is a guarantee from the inspector. When I do a pre-listing inspection, I offer the following promise:

> *I guarantee my inspection like this: if another inspector working for the buyer finds something that I missed that is included in my Standards of Practice, I'll pay for the repairs up to the cost of your inspection.*

Most inspectors are not going to voluntarily offer a guarantee so it's up to you to ask. The best inspectors will have some way of backing up their work. Those are the ones that you want to work with.

Inspector Checklist

Questions to ask Before Hiring an Inspector

- ✓ Is the Inspector Licensed (if required in your state); otherwise, certified?
- ✓ How long have they worked as an Inspector?
- ✓ Approximately how many home inspections do they complete annually?
- ✓ How long will the inspection take?
- ✓ May you (as the owner) attend the inspection? (If the answer is 'No', run!)
- ✓ What type of report will the Inspector provide?
- ✓ Does the Inspector provide free follow up service? For fee?
- ✓ What guarantees does the Inspector provide?
- ✓ Is the Inspector bonded and insured?
- ✓ Does the Inspector have a website where you can locate more information?

Chapter 2—Utilities

If you are currently occupying the home that you are selling, this section may seem foolish at first. The power is already on, as is the water. In fact, everything is on because you are living in the property. Please don't disregard or skip what follows—we have a lot of information in this chapter that will makes things easier on the inspector and set you on a smooth path towards closing.

If you are selling the home while it's vacant, please pay attention to some of the items in the chapter. You may need to rely on your Realtor to assist you in preparing the home for the inspection.

Electrical Services

This may sound obvious but the inspector needs to have the electricity on in order to test a range of home systems: the heating and cooling systems, kitchen appliances, ventilation fans, lights, receptacles, and more. You get the idea. Yet, a common issue inspectors run into is a vacant home where the power has been turned off. This most often occurs with a home that is in foreclosure—banks and HUD are notoriously bad at doing anything to get the home ready. However, sometimes the property is vacant because the sellers have moved to their new abode or are anticipating a fast sale and have not leased the property to new tenants.

Whatever the reason, without power the inspector cannot do a competent job. If the inspector finds the house to be without electricity, he or she will have several options. The first option is to simply mark items as Not Inspected. I warn you right now that although most inspector Standards allow this, the buyer will be displeased with both you and the inspector in that event.

Option 2 will be to recommend having the electrical components energized and then inspected by an electrician. The buyer will certainly expect you to provide the funds for this service.

Option 3 is to see if the inspector is willing to return and complete the inspection once the power is turned on. Expect this to cost an additional fee.

There are some repercussions to each option. Option 1 may kill your deal. The buyer may feel that a failure to provide adequate conditions to inspect is evidence of a seller with something to hide. Options 2 and 3 will cost someone money—and assuredly, hands will stretch in your direction. All of the options lead to unnecessary delays in getting to a closing successfully.

If your electrical service is on and is to remain on, make sure that the electrical panel is easily accessible. All the Standards call for the inspector to remove the service panel cover to inspect the breakers and wiring. None of them mandate the inspector putting his life in jeopardy to do so.

Quick story. While inspecting a house one day, I was taking off the cover of a newer electrical panel. As I removed one of the screws, a rather spectacular sparkler effect burst out from the panel, causing the main breaker to trip, and nearly scaring the inspector (me!) half to death. Believe it or not, enough energy was transferred to weld the screw to the panel cover! What had happened was, unbeknownst to me, an electrician had installed a 50-amp breaker into the panel and folded the excess wire into the bottom of the panel box instead of trimming it back as required. The wire relaxed and expanded — as it is prone to do, one of the reasons it should be trimmed —until it touched the screw. When I removed that screw, it cut across both energized wires.

Fortunately for me, there was suitable access in front of the panel; I wasn't leaning on a washing machine or sitting on a freezer to reach it. I was wearing insulating shoes and using insulated tools, which means I was not physically in contact with the panel.

Please, for the safety of everyone involved, make sure that the panel is accessible. Also ensure that the screws are accessible and that there is room to remove the cover once the screws are withdrawn. There should not be anything placed in front of the panel within 36 inches and there should be at least 30 inches of room to each the side. It would also be nice if we did not have to climb a stack of boxes to reach the panel.

I can assure you that the inspector will not resent a note identifying the location of the electrical panel. In older homes that have seen extensive remodeling, the panels may be hidden. I have also seen many older homes that have built-in decorative boxes to disguise the panel.

Gas Services

Gas must be on and/or propane and oil reserves must be full enough to test the furnace and any appliances (gas stoves, fireplaces, etc.) installed in the home.

If you have cut off the power to your home, you likely turned off the gas as well. For good measure, the utility supplier locks the valve once the gas is shut off and there's not a home inspector in the country that's going to cut that lock. The gas needs to be turned on by the supplier for an adequate inspection to occur.

If you have propane or oil service instead of natural gas, make sure there is enough fuel to test the furnace and any appliances (gas stoves, fireplaces) that are installed in the home.

By code, every gas-fueled appliance is required to have a shut-off valve. Most home inspectors will not operate these due to liability issues. On the day of the inspection, if not sooner, verify that these valves are turned to the ON position. If any of the equipment (usually gas fireplaces) need to have pilots lit, do that as well.

All of the gas valves, from the main one outside to the fireplace and stove valves, need to be accessible. Remove any personal possessions that may block the inspector from each valve. Some valves, such as those on gas ranges, may be behind the unit. Let us know in a note that it's back there and also if it is okay to move the stove. Even with permission, many inspectors will not move the stove but you will at least reassure everyone that the valve does indeed exist.

For the valve on the exterior of the house, consider trimming the shrubs or any other vegetation so we don't have to break out the machete to hack our way in.

Water Services

Water is the single biggest destroyer of homes. Proper maintenance and repair of any leaks, damage, or broken pipes must be verified to protect the client. About once a month, I show up at an inspection and see a little tag from one of our local municipal water companies hanging on the door informing the owner that the water has been turned off. This is not good news for me. First, I know right away that I'm in for a future visit to the home, which makes me slightly cranky. Second, if there are leaks in the sinks or showers, I can't find them. In winter, I worry about broken pipes behind finished surfaces. Without water, these big problems can go undetected.

Utilities Checklist

SERVICES

✓ Electricity is on.

✓ Water is on.

✓ Natural Gas, if present, is on.

✓ If the home has an above-ground oil or propane tank, sufficient fuel is present to run furnace, etc.

✓ All gas appliances have gas valves in the 'ON' position.

✓ All pilot lights are lit (even in summer).

ACCESSIBILITY

✓ Can the electrical panel cover be removed safely? There should be full access to the front and sides, no obstacles in the travel path. If the panel is on the exterior of the home, any locks are removed.

✓ Is there sufficient room in front of the furnace for the inspector to work? Can the covers be safely removed?

✓ Is there sufficient room in front of the water heater for the inspector? Can the covers be removed?

✓ Is there sufficient room in front of the air conditioner for the inspector?

✓ The water main is visible and accessible? If behind a panel, leave the inspector a note on the location.

Chapter 3—Curb Appeal

First Impressions

Use your imagination for a minute and put yourself in the position of the buyer. Your Realtor has told you about a house in your preferred neighborhood that's in your price range–and with that extra half bath you need. Sounds great! Now imagine pulling up in front of your "dream" home at the appointed hour and seeing that the lawn is slightly over-grown, the kiddy pool is upside down, sand is spilling out of a planter all over the front patio, toys are scattered everywhere, a snow shovel is leaning against the garage (in August…), and, last but not least, the raspberry patch looks like a thicket.

If buyers were visiting my house, this is exactly what they would see. Two points in my defense – the grandkids were just over, and I'm not selling my house. If I were, all of those things would be corrected.

Even though the inspector looks at things much differently than your buyers, he is going to be influenced by the first impression of your home. If the outside looks like a mess, the inspector can only imagine what hidden problems lie within your home. Try to ease him or her into the process by maintaining what your agent calls "curb appeal." Make the home attractive to look at, uncluttered, and welcoming.

The Front Yard

The grounds don't have to look like a candidate for the "Beautiful Yard" contest from the local garden club, it just needs to be neat. Start with the basics: water your lawn and greenery often in summer and mow your lawn regularly. A green lawn, even one with a few weeds, evokes a warm response. Trim the shrubs and trees. Planting a few flowers never hurts.

Truthfully, the inspector is not going to care much about the yard unless there are hazards present. Hazards can include easy-to-fix items like holes dug by an eager puppy that could cause someone to trip or bigger items like a koi pond that may be dangerous for small children. In the first case, it is worth taking two minutes out of your day to fill in the holes. In the case of a water feature, the buyer will already be aware of it and is discounting it. As an inspector, I will make a cautionary note about water features even though they are outside the scope of the inspection. After that, it's up to the client to determine their particular level of concern.

If you have abandoned equipment or materials on the lot, get rid of it. Nothing will destroy curb appeal like an old car or stacks of half-rotted lumber that no one has touched in ten years. The same applies to firewood, broken toys and bikes, old boats, paint cans—all need to go. If you want to keep these items for the future, figure out where you can store them off of the property.

Driveways and Walkways

Again, the goal is to take care of the basics. If there are weeds growing in the cracks, remove them or hit them with some weed killer. Larger cracks can be sealed with a concrete caulk or epoxy. If the driveway is asphalt, you can apply a sealer to the surface such as Latex-ite's Acrylic Plus Driveway Revitalizer Filler/Sealer.

Holes in an asphalt driveway should be filled with a cold patch. It's inexpensive and will improve the look of the driveway while limiting future damage. If you have an edge that is breaking down due to poor compaction when the driveway was put in, you'll have to live with it.

Likewise, smaller holes in concrete driveways can be patched but I would not waste effort if you have a concrete driveway exhibiting surface spalling. (*Spalling occurs in concrete when moisture penetrates the surface and goes through freeze/thaw cycles and small sections and rocks are popped out. Because the condition tends to affect the concrete to only a shallow depth, repairs are similarly thin and deteriorate rapidly.*)

There isn't much you can do if the driveway is in very poor condition since repairs at this point would include a full replacement, which is well beyond what we're trying to accomplish here. The good news is that most driveways are usable in their current condition and most buyers just want a flat spot to park the car.

Walkways have the same issues as driveways but introduce trip hazards to the mix. A trip hazard is an area where the walkway has settled or heaved and left an edge exposed that can catch the toe of a pedestrian. There are a couple of ways to handle trip hazards depending on how aggressive you want to be. The easiest thing to do is to simply ignore it. Most people will already have seen the trip hazard when they did the initial visit and will have accounted for it. If you intend to fix it, you have two options for concrete walkways.

The first is to apply a patch and create a beveled surface that will cause the foot to skim up to the high point in the walkway. To do this, start by cleaning the walkway thoroughly then apply a high-quality, high strength concrete patch to the affected area. This option is the fastest and easiest repair but will need to be re-done every couple of years in areas that have severe winter weather.

The second option is to grind the surface down to make a level path. Most people have seen this method even if they're not cognizant of it. The public walkways that are maintained by municipalities often use this approach to create a more level surface. By using a concrete grinder, you can take the high edge down and make a smooth transition. The grinders are expensive to buy though so you'll be looking at renting one. I'll warn you now that it is a noisy and dirty process.

Make sure to remove any temporary obstructions, like toys, from the walkway before the inspector gets there. If it snowed, shovel a path from the sidewalk or driveway to your door. It makes it safer for everybody who needs to enter your home and will limit how much snow gets tracked into the home.

Steps, Stoops, and Porches

There are a few considerations when we look at the steps and stoops leading into the home. The most common defect for steps and stoops is a missing handrail. A handrail is required when there are four or more steps present or when the surface of the landing is 30-inches above grade. I have had several banks insist on upgrading the handrail as part of the underwriting process, however it's rare for buyers to request this.

It is not unusual for older homes to exhibit considerable settlement at the stoops. As long as the settlement is not impacting the foundation of the home, the inspector will generally note it but not recommend replacement due to the high cost. If the steps themselves are deteriorating, plan on patching them.

Check your screen door and landings, especially on older homes. Many of the landings in older homes were made much smaller than the 36"x 36" platform that is now required. Often, I'll point out to buyers that when the screen door opens, anyone standing on the steps is in danger of being knocked backwards. For adults it is not much of concern, but smaller children can be seriously injured with even a short fall down concrete steps. Also, make sure that the screens are in good condition. You are better off removing a screen door than leaving one with a severely ripped screen or damaged frame.

Grading at the Foundation

Grading refers to the slope of the ground at your foundation. Is the soil higher by the house than the rest of lot (within 10 feet of the walls) and how close is the soil to your siding.

Take a look at the perimeter of your home. Specifically, look to see how close the soil comes to touching your siding. If soil is right up against the siding, inspectors will automatically call out a lack of clearance here. Oftentimes, the issue originated with a landscaper (in a new home) who built beautiful beds next to the house but didn't remove excess soil to maintain the necessary clearance prior to adding the planting materials.

If you can, remove excess soil to give your siding 4-6 inches of clearances. I don't walk around with a ruler to measure the actual amount of clearance—that seems a bit excessive—but help the inspector out by giving him a reason to say, "Good enough."

Another issue, one that directly affects the manner in which water flows, might be that you have negative grade, meaning that the soil slopes toward your home instead of away from it. This may not be easy to correct because just adding to the level of the soil, may cause an issue with the clearance. If that's the case, just leave it.

Older homes may have subsided into the soil and have a "bathtub" effect on the full perimeter. Unless you are willing to shift large amounts of dirt, let the inspector call it. The issue of concern in this instance is water runoff towards the foundation. I have some other suggestions, found in the Roofing section, that will help with this item.

Considerations that Fall Out of the Scope of Inspection

Fences, mailboxes, lawn decorations, and landscaping features are usually not part of the inspection. Still, many inspectors will comment on a fence that is in poor repair (plus, it hurts the curb appeal of your home). Replacing the fence is not usually feasible but you should make efforts to shore up sections that are leaning and get gates working properly.

In the area that I practice, pools are uncommon. In areas such as Florida, Nevada, and California, the backyard pool is a staple of comfortable living. If you have a pool, I strongly recommend that you have the pool serviced by a specialist and have the entire system checked for safety issues. Also note that the electrical codes have changed substantially in the last several years. You'll want to make sure you are ready to deal with those. Also note that pool fences have their own special requirements. This will be something that varies by region.

If you have a sprinkler system, run it through the cycles and make a note of which zone serves which area. Again, this is an add-on for some inspection companies but most buyers will want to know the system is in good repair. Have any broken heads repaired and get the heads adjusted to make sure none of them are spraying on the house or deck supports. I routinely identify wooden posts that have rot at the base because the sprinkler system has been soaking them every summer since 1988. Make sure this isn't the case at your home.

Curb Appeal Checklist

Look at your home from the street. . .

- ✓ Decide if you are doing any repairs to the driveway or walkway. If so, complete before the inspection. Otherwise, negotiate it through your Realtor.
- ✓ Keep the lawn green and mowed. Mow the day before the inspection.
- ✓ Are all toys, tools, etc. removed from walkways?
- ✓ If you have a dog, please clean up the yard just before the inspection.
- ✓ Trim bushes, etc., to provide access around the perimeter of the home.
- ✓ Fill in any holes in the yard with soil.
- ✓ Unlock all outbuildings. They may not be included in the inspection but the buyers will want to look.
- ✓ Review grading and soil clearance around your homes foundation and siding
- ✓ If you have a pool, hire a specialist to inspect and make any needed repairs.
- ✓ If you have in-ground sprinklers, are they working and adjusted properly?
- ✓ If you have screen doors, are they in good condition?

Chapter 4 – Exteriors

The exterior of the home—the siding and roof—frequently get mentioned along with the word "repair" in the inspection report. We can't possibly cover every single possibility in a guide such as this but it's important to hit some of the highlights.

First, a cautionary statement: you are almost always better off leaving an exterior problem alone rather than do a poor job of repair yourself. A poor repair that looks as though it might be a cover-up endangers the trust you have sought to build with your buyer. If you are not competent to perform the repairs, either hire someone who is or wait to negotiate it.

Siding

Two issues present themselves with siding. The first is that poor materials that are not well installed can be a deal breaker. I had one client who was adamant that he would not buy a home with LP (Louisiana Pacific) siding because a particular type of the LP siding products manufactured in the mid- to late-80s and into the 90s had substantial problems with degradation due to water intrusion. The problems were bad enough that LP ended up in court and lost a class action suit. (The deadline to file claims was December 31, 2002.)

At least a half-dozen different companies have been in litigation regarding their siding. If you have a type of siding that is of questionable quality, be prepared to discuss it. Recognize that your home is not the only one with these types of siding. The inspector will report troublesome siding only when he or she can definitively identify it. This is challenging as the markings that indicate the siding are on the back and cannot be seen without removing the planks, which is well beyond the scope of the inspection.

Another type of siding that is problematic is the old cement asbestos shingles used in the 1940s and 1950s. I actually like this product a lot as a siding. It's durable, holds paint well, and has a pleasing appearance. The concern is the little asbestos fibers. These fibers are not generally a health hazard as long as the siding is in good condition (See Chapter 10 for more information regarding asbestos) but it can raise the cost to perform any repairs on the exterior if the siding needs to be cut.

The point is that unless you are willing to invest a substantial sum of money re-siding your home, money that you will not recover in the transaction, the siding you have is the siding we deal with. The most important thing you can do is to take a breath while we move onto siding maintenance.

The second issue commonly found when it comes to siding applies to all siding products—general maintenance. Start by looking at your siding and considering the paint. If the paint coverage is worn and faded, it may be time to repaint. If the paint is in generally good condition, look carefully for spots that will need a touch-up.

Obviously, if the paint is in very poor condition, you have a choice to make. Repainting will definitely take a hit on your wallet but you may take a larger hit on your home's sale price if left undone. Before you make a decision, talk to your agent about their recommendations and be forthcoming about your expectations. If you want top dollar for your home, it will need to be in turnkey condition and that includes the siding.

If you decide to do maintenance painting, match the paint color as closely as you can. The human eye is a remarkable organ and can spot differences in color, texture, and sheen at a threshold that might surprise you. Take a chip of the color to the local hardware store to get an exact match. Most now have analyzers that will look at the chip and generate a matching tint.

Before you paint, check any woodwork for rot. Remember that comment about trust I made a minute ago? The most common cover-up I see on the exterior is a heavy layer of paint on deteriorating wood or wood composite. Instead of taking a gamble and potentially disrupting that hard-earned trust, spend a few dollars to replace rotted or severely weathered trim.

If you have a stone or brick façade, look for missing mortar or cracks in the joints that need to be sealed or repainted. I generally recommend hiring this job out. A bad mortar job really attracts the eye—which is exactly the opposite of what we want!

Doors and Windows

Your buyers are going to be in and out of every door and testing every window. Make sure that everything is in good working order! All doors should open smoothly. Knobs should turn easily and the mechanisms should engage without having to lift on the handle or jam a shoulder into the door panel to get it to latch.

Take special care to look at the area immediately surrounding exterior doors. Door casings often need to be repainted and are also a prime culprit for water damage and rot. Ditto for the thresholds.

The windows should be in tip-top shape and easy to operate. On the exterior, the inspector is checking the trim and sills for cracks and damage, and looking for broken panes, damaged thermal seals, and the condition of any glazing. I recommend you repairing any windows issues. If you have older single pane windows that need the glazing repaired, do it. Scrape and paint any peeling paint on the trim or sills. Replace broken panes of glass.

Also check the integrity of all caulk joints around the windows, doors, and trim. A failure in this area leads to water damage, which is especially noticeable in composite sidings. It also introduces watermarks in the interior of the home—which is guaranteed to generate excitement. We prefer boredom.

The Roof

Standard warning alert —if you are not comfortable on the elevated surfaces, are prone to dizzy spells, have poor balance, or are generally unlucky—please do not get on your roof. Hire a handyman instead.

Now, moving on ... *carefully*.

We are not going to contemplate major roof repairs or replacement. If you need those, the roofing contractor will take care of all the other items that we'll cover.

Gutters

First things first, are your gutters clean? In older communities, the gutters need cleaning at least annually and often 2-3 times per year. This needs to be done as it is an automatic call on the part of the inspector and one of the most commonly requested repair items. (Also remove all tennis balls and kids toys from the gutters. My record for tennis balls is seven from one home. Somebody had a lousy arm.)

Now that the gutters are clean, go look to see if they move water away from the foundation or discharge it against the home. New homes will be connected (usually) to the municipal storm water drainages via underground connections. Older homes should have splashblocks, gutter extensions, or other systems that will direct water as far from the home as possible. Be sure these are clear of any obstructions and are clean.

Roof Deck

Now shift your focus to the roof itself. Are there any missing or damaged shingles? If so, get someone up there to replace them. Nothing scares a buyer quite so much as a feeling that the roof is about to fail and leak all over the house. One missing shingle is enough to trigger this response.

Remove all organic debris, like small branches and leaves that can accumulate. The presence of the debris triggers an "it's old and failing" response even if the underlying shingles are in reasonably good shape. Moss should be removed as well. Remember to treat the roots or someone will have to do it again in a couple of years.

Do not use a pressure washer to remove the debris and moss! Instead, use a push broom and sweep in a downward motion to prevent damage to the shingles.

Now think about how the debris got up there in the first place. Probably a tree, right? Trim any branches that are rubbing on the shingles and remove dead branches that may be ready to drop from overhanging trees.

While you're on the roof, look for nails pushing up on the shingles. This is fairly common. The repair is reasonably easy. First, lift the shingle to expose the head of the nail, and then use a claw hammer to remove the offender. Drive another nail about one inch from the original. Seal both the resulting hole and the tar strip along the edge of the overlapping shingle with an approved roofing mastic.

So far, I've made the assumption that your roof covering is a traditional asphalt composition shingle, whether a three tab or architectural style. Much of the above advice also applies to wood shake, metal, and membrane roofs. Concrete tile and slate roofs will have some additional requirements.

The good news is that these roof coverings tend to be much more durable, so the repairs tend to be minor unless we're at the end of the lifespan for the material.

Other than basic cleaning, I recommend hiring roofing contractors that specialize in the materials do any necessary repairs. Roof flashing is tricky to work with and can lead to leaks if not installed properly. Also, regional standards vary, so what may appear incorrect to your eyes may actually be considered acceptable by the roofers and inspectors. Punt on this one and hire a roofing contractor with insurance.

A roof that is in poor repair will almost certainly cause you aggravation, either by encouraging the buyer to walk away or by having an addendum submitted that will request repairs or replacement. Be prepared for either.

Exteriors Checklist

PAINT AND SIDING

- ✓ Check exterior wood for rot prior to painting.
- ✓ Replace weather-damaged or rotted materials.
- ✓ Touch-up paint.
- ✓ Check all caulking and repair as necessary.

DOORS AND WINDOWS

- ✓ Test doors and windows for operation. Repair where possible.
- ✓ Repair any damaged window glazing.
- ✓ Door and window hardware in good operating condition. All the windows lock.

ROOF

- ✓ Clean the gutters. Install splashblocks if needed.
- ✓ Remove all organic debris, including moss.
- ✓ Repair any loose or missing shingles. Re-set nails.
- ✓ Seal all exposed nails.
- ✓ If the roof is aging, consider getting an estimate on remaining life from a roofing expert.

Chapter 5 – Interiors

Let's move inside your home. As with the other sections, I'm not advocating for major repairs. Some small repairs and a bit of common sense usually results in a smooth process for the inspector and helps to preserve that all-important trust you're developing with the buyer.

Clean Your House

The simple truth of the matter is that an inspector will scrutinize a home more closely if the interior is in shambles. I don't mean normal, day-to-day living clutter. I mean homes where I could not inspect the floor because it was covered two feet deep in clothes, toys, books, etc.

Or frat houses where you could hear the sucking sound from the soles of my shoes as I walked across the beery floors.

Or the home I didn't dare take off my shoes (I hate to mess up people's homes with dirty shoes) because the carpet was strewn with pet feces.

These are extreme examples, I admit, but the larger point remains—if the inspector is in an environment that suggests that basic cleanliness isn't maintained, it's a short leap of logic to guess that the big things haven't been done either. Err on the side of caution and dedicate a cleaning day (or two…) to make sure your home is ready for company.

Now for specifics.

Family room and bedrooms

If you de-cluttered as your Realtor suggested (and they will all suggest it) you should be ready. If not, start with the floors. Make sure the floors are clear of obstructions. I'm talking about dirty clothes that should be in baskets or shifted to the laundry room. For those that have young children, toys should be corralled into bins or shelves as best as possible. I understand that the average toddler can deploy all their toys three times faster than a parent can pick them up, but please try.

The inspector will work around packing boxes, but keep them organized and leave clear walking paths. If you put them up against a wall, the inspector will likely mark this area as 'Not inspected' in the report. If the other areas look to be in good repair, this won't be a problem. If, however, there is an issue with the wall such as a water stain or hole, leave it visible. Never allow yourself to be accused of covering something up.

If you have water stains on the ceiling, be prepared to answer some questions. A simple statement on when the stain was noticed and why or where it came from (if applicable) are all that is necessary. If they were there prior to your occupancy, expect to prove it via the home inspection you commissioned when you purchased the house.

If you have large hanging tapestries, consider removing them. Likewise, any decorative fabrics attached to the ceiling should be removed. Most often, I see these in the rooms of teenagers to create mood, but they limit effective observations of the ceiling and are generally a turn-off to homebuyers.

The inspector is required to test a representative number of windows and doors. Please make sure that they are in good operating condition and are accessible. If the window is a casement style, make sure all the cranks are present and work. Leave space directly in front of windows to improve access and remove any fragile items you might have on the windowsill or sitting in front of a window. The inspector will make every effort to avoid disturbing your possessions. (Speaking for myself, I'd rather write up a window as untested than risk breaking one of your prized glass figurines.) Try to leave the curtains open and if you have blinds, raise them. It will speed up the inspection and provide much needed light to the room being inspected.

The doors should not have hanging racks, backpacks, or clothes hangers that block the normal operation of the door.

Make sure that electrical receptacles (outlets and/or sockets) can be tested in each room. The inspector is not required to test all of them (though I try) but he or she does need to test a representative number.

The diffusers (heating/cooling vents) should be visible. When you're staging your home for sale, you might consider this and rearrange the furniture. For example, if the couch is sitting on top them, pull the couch away from the wall for the time being.

Turn on the lights and any fans. The inspector should be considerate enough to turn them off as they finish the inspection.

On a more personal note, if you have items that you do not want to share with potential buyers due to their intimate nature, please put them in drawers where no one will see them. I apologize if this embarrasses anyone, but after a decade of doing inspections I've discovered that people forget that not everyone possesses the same degree of comfort with certain types of personal items. This also applies to substances that might be considered illegal outside the state of Washington where I work.

Kitchens

The kitchen is the figurative heart of the home. Make it as inviting as possible.

Kitchens pose special problems for the inspector because there are a large number of items to inspect, including the appliances. Approximately half the inspectors write the report at the house and they need a spot to set up their computer. The kitchen counter is a favorite due to its central location, the (usually) abundant receptacles, and the opportunity to test appliances and water supplies while typing.

When prepping for the inspector, first clear the countertops and wipe them down. A sticky surface will negatively affect the buyer and inspector alike. In the case of the buyers, they may not even realize the effect that a minor mess has on them. I can assure you that after observing about four thousand buyers, I know that they react more strongly in the kitchen than any other room, except the bathroom.

Do the dishes. The sinks should be empty and rinsed of any food particles. Dishes should be put away or stacked neatly in a drainer if you hand wash.

One exception: the dishwasher. The inspector will be testing this appliance (it's a primary source of leaks in the kitchen and an appliance that is subject to frequent failure). If you have dirty dishes, rinse them, put them in the dishwasher with dishwashing soap, and leave me a note: *"The dishwasher is ready to go, just turn it on."* Cue instant trust for this appliance! You can also load it and have it running when I arrive. If the washer comes with a delay feature, use it to match the time of the inspection.

If your house is vacant because you have already moved, have your agent run the dishwasher the day before. If not used regularly, the dishwasher can lose prime on the pump and make an awful grinding sound. Better to have that corrected and out of earshot before inspection! Pouring a cup of water into the dishwasher usually helps to reestablish the prime.

The surface of the stove should be clean and pots removed. A teapot can be left on as decoration. The inspector will remove it to test the burners but the image conveys warmth. Make sure the teapot is clean on the outside.

The oven should also be clean and ready to be turned ON. If you store pots and pans in your oven, consider a different option for the day of the inspection. Not every inspector will check to make sure the oven is empty, which can lead to damage to your cookery, and most will not unload the oven due to time constraints. Pizza stones, grill pans, and roasters can be left in but I don't recommended it.

Please clean your refrigerator. It doesn't need to be spotless but it should be orderly with all the shelving and drawers intact. If the house is vacant, leave the refrigerator off with the door(s) open to limit mildew/mold growth. Thoroughly wipe the interior to remove the last of the moisture. I would prefer that you leave it plugged in as I am reluctant to risk damaging the flooring by trying to drag the refrigerator out to reach the plug.

If there is a built-in microwave, clean the interior (including the inside top) and give the exterior a wipe down.

The range hood may be built into the microwave or be a separate hood assembly. Both types will have screens to filter the air that need to be cleaned (it actually should be done on a regular basis).

Under the sink, the inspector will need to be able to see all the supply and drainage plumbing. Plastic bags, trash cans, bottles and boxes of cleaners, and a dozen other items can make this a challenge. Remove as much as possible from this area, even if it means placing it in a box discreetly stored in another part of the kitchen.

Bathrooms

As I mentioned above, the bathrooms are the most sensitive areas from a cleanliness perspective. The visceral reaction occurs below the level of conscious thought, though I can often read it on client's faces. Putting it bluntly, a dirty bathroom can ruin your hope of selling your home, even if the inspection comes back with minor items.

All counters, vanities, and sinks should be wiped down. The sink cabinet should be cleared out and cleaned up.

Major areas of concern are the condition of the floor, the commode, and the tub.

First, make sure that all the commodes were flushed before the inspector gets to your home. This is doubly important if you have young children still in the training phases of bathroom etiquette. The exterior surfaces should be wiped clean. Use a cleaning agent and brush to improve the bowl. It doesn't need to be spotless, just clean. Minor hard water deposits will not create an adverse reaction.

Tubs and shower enclosures should have all the bottles and soaps neatly stored. Remove washcloths. The interior of the enclosure should be clean. If there is hair present (having raised three girls with long hair, I've become acquainted with hair issues) remove it. If you are storing toys, cat food, a litter box, or boots in the tub, take them out for the day. I suggest leaving shower curtains open, shower doors closed.

The floor should be swept and mopped prior to the inspection. The area around the commode is the most important. You'll want to make sure that you clean all the way to the wall, not just in front.

Towels should either be hung neatly or removed to the laundry. Hanging them neatly, especially if they are attractive towels, will enhance the appearance of the bathrooms.

Fast and Easy Repairs

The following categories are placed in identical order as the sections above to make coordination a bit easier for you. Some of this will be repeated in the checklist at the end of the chapter.

Family Room and Bedrooms

If you have removed a painting or pictures from the walls, fill in any holes from nails or tacks. If you have removed a large screen television that hung from large mollies, you may wish to bring in a handyman to patch the holes.

New buyers will question straight-line cracks in the ceilings and walls. Most cracking is typical for the types of materials used and is a result of the minor settlement that every home undergoes as well as the thermal expansion and contraction that takes place seasonally. If you intend to paint, and you should, fill these thin cracks with a paintable caulk using a small amount of sealant on your finger and working it into the crack. This works well for homes with standard drywall construction. Lathe and plaster walls can be more difficult to work. Plaster walls are also more prone to cracking. A good inspector will inform the clients that the cracking is typical even if you do not repair it.

Be more cautious with larger cracks, especially if the crack extends at a jagged diagonal across the wall. This is symptomatic of foundational issues and is a big indicator that it's time to call in an expert, either an inspector for a limited inspection or a foundation contractor.

Clean the windows, the sills, and the tracks. There is an excellent chance that your Realtor suggested removing the screens from the windows. They did so because the screens limit light transference, and removing them makes your home look brighter and more cheerful. So leave them off, but also leave the buyers and inspector a note that the screens have been removed, where they are stored, and when you intend to reinstall them. If you have damaged screens, either identify it or repair it.

Patch any small holes in your doors. Large holes will require replacement of the whole door. It's relatively inexpensive, so consider it. All the doors should open and close smoothly, with properly working hardware. This includes the closet doors. Make sure all the closet doors are present and on their tracks. If you have removed them, which I see often in homes with smaller children, leave a note on where you have them stored and whether you intend to re-hang them.

If any light bulbs are burned out, replace them. It's much better (and cheaper!) for you to nip this problem in the bud. Don't wait for the inspector to note that a light fixture wasn't working at the time of the inspection and recommend repairs by a licensed electrician.

The same applies to missing or broken cover plates for switches and receptacles. Even if the crack is minor, consider replacing the plate. Switches in older homes get wobbly and the receptacles get loose enough that plugs will fall out. All of these should be replaced.

Assess your skills honestly and decide if you wish to tackle this yourself or hire it out. In many jurisdictions, the repairs will need to be done by a licensed electrician. If all the receptacles and switches in the whole house are at issue, as is the case in a fair number of 1940's bungalows, you may wish to wait for the buyer to request the repairs.

Interiors 35

You probably cleaned your floors prior to listing the house. That's good. Check to see if small spot cleaning is necessary. If the carpet is excessively worn or the wood floors are in need of refinishing, I would not expend any substantial effort to upgrade this. If the buyers put in an offer, they've already accounted (and probably discounted) for the floors.

The same applies to painting. If you didn't do this prior to listing, don't do it now. Pre-listing, painting the walls creates a fresh and clean impression that pleases the buyers. Post-offer, it disturbs their mental image of the home, and more importantly, the mental exercises buyers do as they plan their lives in "their home."

Kitchens

The kitchen has a couple of "musts" that you will need to address.

First, if your home is pre-1976 and the outlets have not been updated, you will need to get GFCI's (Ground Fault Circuit Interrupter) receptacles installed. These are the ones with the Test/Reset buttons in them. If the kitchen lacks these, the inspector (and appraiser) will mark them for repair, so you might as well be ahead of this one.

Second, if you have any leaks under the sink, get them fixed properly. You can test for leaks yourself by simply filling the sinks with water and removing the stopper. Don't rely on your eyes to find a leak. Run a hand around each fitting and then look at your fingertips after each fitting for dampness. If you find dampness, you have a leak. Obviously, if water is dripping, fix that first.

A trend in my area has been for homeowners to replace all the traps under the sinks prior to inspection. This clears out slow drains, plus the new materials present a better image to the buyers and the inspector. Consider doing it.

Now, let's go through the kitchen, looking at each component.

Sinks

Depending on the surface, there's little to do—assuming that the faucets and drainage are working well. If the faucet is leaky or looks as though it was installed during the Eisenhower administration, replace it. If there are an excessive number of chips or scratches in your sink, think about replacing it. Usually, if this is the case, you're going to have issues with the counters and cabinetry, too. Read on.

Cabinets

All the doors and drawers should have pulls unless the style does not require it. Don't have half with and half without. The buyer, primarily the woman, will add dollars to the missing hardware. You need a full complement of pulls and knobs. Tighten any that are loose.

All the hardware needs to function smoothly. Drawers should slide open with minimum effort and cabinet doors should fit together cleanly. If the drawers are difficult to open, look at the tracks and see if cleaning them will help. Most do not require lubrication so don't oil them. The stains from drips—and it will drip—is a turnoff.

Look over your cabinets. The hinges should be tight and working well. Cabinet doors that are off-center with one door visibly higher than the other when closed calls into question the relative quality of the cabinet and the workmanship. Adjust as much as possible to have an even line along the bottom edge of the cabinet doors.

If you have damaged wood in the base cabinet below the sink from a leak, get it fixed or resurfaced.

Dated cabinetry leaves you with three choices: You can leave them as is, you can refinish them, or you can replace them. Refinishing must be done in a professional manner or the net effect will be worse than if you went with the as-is scenario. If painting, the colors should be neutral and natural. Black and white paint schemes with vivid red accruements may look very slick in the magazine, but will widen the eyes of the buyers–and not in a manner that conveys happy emotions.

Countertops

Don't chase the newest big thing in countertops. If your counters have acceptable surfaces, just clean, caulk, and clear them. It's not necessary to replace your attractive and functional counters to go with the latest in marble, tile or concrete styles unless the goal is improved salability. It probably will not make the home sale more profitable, but trading dollars for speed of sale is definitely worth considering. Just be cognizant of the reason for the change.

If the counters are in poor condition, you can replace them with a laminate surface or a range of materials, including Corian and tile. Discuss with your Realtor the trends in your specific region. When I left San Diego, entry-level homes had white tile counters. A decade later, those counters are now considered dated.

Caulk the intersection of the backsplash and the countertop. Use clear silicon caulk for this.

Appliances

If you are living in the home, you'll need functional appliances but that doesn't mean that you need to leave them for the new owner. Homes get sold with ancient appliances, mismatched sets, sparkling new pieces, and everything in between.

Decide ahead of time if you are taking the refrigerator with you or the new stove. Disclose this up front with potential buyers so they can then budget for that. If you are selling an entry-level home, think about leaving the appliances or offering an allowance for the purchase of new equipment. Most first-time homebuyers are entering into the deal with low cash reserves. Making this kind of reassurance can go a long way in building confidence as they put in the offer and head to the inspection.

If your appliances are used but serviceable, do a routine cleaning of the surfaces and a deep cleaning in the oven as suggested in the last section.

Bathrooms

Once again, the bathroom is a crucial area. Follow the basics in the bathroom. Clean, as mentioned above, and fix any leaks.

Toilets

Check the toilet to make sure that the base is tightened and won't wobble. If it does, try tightening the nuts on either side of the base. DO NOT overtighten. At the same time, check the reservoir for movement. The nuts for these (usually butterfly nuts) are under the flange of the toilet base on either side of the center point.

Fixtures

If all the fixtures — tub, sink, toilet — are avocado green, rose/pink, or mustard yellow, consider upgrading. Talk to the Realtor about your options to see if it improves salability or offer size.

Shower and Tub Enclosures

Re-caulk the entire shower enclosure, including along the floor with the bottom of the shower or the tub reaches the flooring material, with clean silicon. Any missing grout or loose tiles need to be repaired or replaced.

Look for signs that the shower has leaked around the curtain or door, a common occurrence when kids live in the home, and decide whether you wish to replace any visible damage or acknowledge it ahead of time. The buyer probably already noted it and the inspector will put it in the report. On a dollar and cents basis, you might not recover the cost to fix or replace. Unless the damage is an eyesore, versus some minor swelling or bubbling of the surface, I would leave it alone and wait to see if a request is made for repair. In the meantime, get that area dried out. The fear factor goes up quite a bit if the inspector lays a moisture meter on the spot and it squeals.

Make sure the curtain or door is in good repair. Both should be clean and free of mildew and excessive watermarks or soap stains.

Old fixtures detract from the overall appearance and leak at a higher rate than newer faucets. Modern handles and faucets gleam in the lights. Older ones look crusty. Which would you rather have in a house you are buying?

If the subfloor material got wet and has swelled, or if the flooring is exceptionally worn, consider more in depth repairs. Otherwise, a fast touch up will work just fine! If you have tile floors, check the condition of the grout. Small rips or tears in vinyl aren't unusual and your time can be better spent fixing a more immediate problem than resurfacing the entire bathroom for one small defect. Let the inspector call it. If the buyer insists a replacement, use it for negotiating.

Miscellaneous

The mirror and medicine cabinet should be intact. Clean the glass the day of the inspection. No one wants to see toothpaste or hairspray splattered on a mirror. Also be mindful that buyers and the inspector will likely be opening your medicine cabinet to inspect the condition of the shelves and function of the door. If there's anything in there you don't want public, find a different spot for it for the day.

Clean the ventilation fan, both the cover and the fan itself. Dirty fans don't move enough air and make weird noises. Some sound like baby Cessna engines. Almost all the newer fan covers (within the last thirty years or so) detach with spring clips. Replace covers that are missing on the fan or the light.

If the bathroom does not have a fan but does have an operable window, you meet the current Standard. The important word is "operable," as a window that cannot be opened is not useful for venting the moisture of the bathroom to the exterior. Anticipate that the inspector will note the lack of a fan and recommend upgrading, even if it meets Standard.

As with the kitchen, if your home is pre-1976 and the outlets have not been updated, you will need to get GFCI's (Ground Fault Circuit Interrupter) receptacles installed.

Family and Bedrooms Checklist

✓ De-clutter everything! Make sure the floor is clear.

✓ Patch small holes and cracks. Prepare statements if a previous leak is present.

✓ Consider repainting if the walls are excessively scuffed or otherwise a detraction. Follow your Realtor's advice on colors.

✓ Remove large tapestries, especially if on the ceiling.

✓ Make sure the interior doors have well-functioning hardware – hinges and knobs.

✓ Make sure the windows move smoothly. Remove any decorations on the sills.

✓ Clean the floors as necessary. A full carpet cleaning may be needed, but the buyers often will accept that from you after you move out.

✓ Make sure the windows move smoothly. Remove any decorations on the sills.

✓ Replace any broken or missing diffusers on the heating ducts.

✓ Install a smoke detector in every bedroom and one per floor, including the basement. Check the batteries or simple replace them all.

✓ Install a carbon monoxide detector if you have a fireplace, gas-fired appliances, or attached garage.

Bathrooms Checklist - Cleaning

- ✓ De-clutter the countertops.
- ✓ Wipe down counters, sinks, vanities.
- ✓ Remove non-essential items from the base cabinet.
- ✓ Clean the floor, especially in the area of the commode.
- ✓ Flush the toilet.
- ✓ Store shampoo and soaps neatly in the shower enclosure. Remove wash cloths.
- ✓ Hang towels on racks, or stack neatly on countertop.

Bathrooms Checklist - Repairs

- ✓ Test the toilet to ensure it is secure. Slight movement is okay. Tighten if necessary.
- ✓ Re-caulk the enclosures as needed.
- ✓ Check the shower curtain/door for condition. Repair or replace as necessary.
- ✓ Discuss replacing faucets, etc. with your Realtor. If leaking, just replace.
- ✓ Make sure the sink and tub drain properly. If not, remove clogs.
- ✓ Re-caulk the sink and backsplash as necessary.
- ✓ Clean the ventilation fans.
- ✓ Replace any burned out light bulbs.
- ✓ Install GFCI's if not already present.

Kitchen Checklist - Cleaning

✓ De-clutter the countertops. Any appliances (mixers, etc.) not used should be removed and stored elsewhere.

✓ Wipe down counters, sinks, the stove, and the fronts of the dishwasher and the refrigerator.

✓ Clean the screen on the range hood. Give the top a wipe with hot, soapy water.

✓ Remove non-essential items from the sink base cabinet.

✓ Make sure the sinks are empty.

✓ Do a fast sweep/mop of the floor (if needed.)

✓ To protect your privacy, consider removing bills, check books, and other personal documents to a secure location.

✓ If you do have dirty dishes, place them in the dishwasher. Add soap and a note if you would like the inspector to "do the dishes."

Kitchen Checklist - Repairs

- ✓ Repair any leaks at the faucet or the drains below the counter.
- ✓ Re-caulk the backsplash as needed.
- ✓ Replace any missing cabinet door/drawer pulls. Fix any hardware (hinges, etc.) that is not functioning correctly.
- ✓ If cabinet doors or drawers are missing, replace them.
- ✓ Re-grout counter tiles tops if needed.
- ✓ Replace any burned out light bulbs.
- ✓ Install GFCI's if not already present.
- ✓ Tighten loose handles on stoves, microwave, and refrigerator.

Chapter 6 - Plumbing

I have no intention of advising you to re-plumb your entire home. Unless you are planning on radical repairs or have an exceedingly old home with archaic fixtures (which I do), everything in this plumbing section can be accomplished by the average home owner. If you are not modestly handy, don't have time, or your home has old fixtures, I suggest hiring a good handyman or plumber. In some jurisdictions, a handyman may not legally be able to perform the plumbing repairs you need. Discuss this with your Realtor.

Now, let's perform a couple of simple tests before the inspection. If you had a pre-listing inspection, your inspector would have already done these.

Fixtures

Sinks

Start by testing the water at every sink in the house. That includes the kitchen sink, all of the bathroom sinks, the utility sink, any sinks at wet bars—all of them. Turn on the taps one at a time, making sure that the hot water tap is on the left hand side (yes, there is actually a code that requires this and some inspector Standards mandate verifying). If the hot water tap is on the *right* hand side that means that the lines below the sink were installed in reverse. Correcting this should be as simple as taking the existing lines and switching them to the correct orientation. Use plumber's tape or have a compression fitting to minimize leaks.

Next, let's test the stopper mechanism or drain plug. Stop the drain and run water. Does it work? Is the water staying in the sink? If not, it is likely that the small lever at the back of the drain pipe under the cabinet is slipping. Readjusting or reconnecting the arm to the lever should repair this. If the sink is older and doesn't have a stopper mechanism, make sure that a stopper is available. We need to fill the sink at least halfway to do the next test.

Keep the sink plugged and fill it at least halfway. Cold water works just fine for this test. You can fill it to the overflow (that little hole up near the rim of the sink) but my experience is that a large percentage of these will leak so it's best to avoid using it.

Once the sink is halfway filled, release the water and look for two things. First, how fast is the water draining? It should be a rapid process with a vortex forming early. If the drain does not cooperate and takes more than a few seconds to form the vortex, the P-trap below the counter is likely clogged with hair, toothpaste, or hair bands (again, I raised girls – it's amazing how many of those end up in the trap).

I do NOT recommend using harsh chemicals like many of the commercial products available at the home improvement store. Depending on your pipe materials, these can cause damage. Instead, remove the trap and clean it. Make sure you have a bucket below the trap when you remove it to catch standing water. I suggest wearing latex or neoprene gloves (you'll be glad you did!).

The second thing to look for is a leak. Leaks are much easier to spot when the riser pipe is full. When the water flow comes down one side of the drain pipe, a leak that might exist on the opposite side of a pipe or union (where two pipes connect) will not activate. Some inspectors won't perform this test but, but if they do you don't want a plumbing surprise waiting. Do the test yourself first and be forewarned.

Baths

The testing here is the same as for sinks but with the added issue of a showerhead. First, test the Hot and Cold handles. If the hot and cold get reversed here, it is a much bigger repair as the valves for the faucet sit behind the shower enclosure walls.

Next fill the tub half full and check that the stopper mechanism or drain plug work. Then, with the water still on, pop on the shower diverter. Look for small leaks around the connection from the showerhead to the supply piping that comes out from the wall. It wouldn't hurt to test the supply pipe; it shouldn't move when you try to jiggle it. If it does, it needs to be better secured within the wall.

Supply Piping

Supply piping is what delivers water from "behind" your walls to your faucets (sinks, tub, shower, etc.). There is very little that you can do with the supply piping prior to the inspection. If you think that you want to spend the money to upgrade this component, realize that the return on your investment may not cover the cost of repairs. The simple truth is that, the only categories for supply piping are "working" and "not working." The buyers *expect* the piping to be in workable condition. If it is, then you're good.

So, keep it simple. Look at the visible plumbing lines. If something is leaking, fix it. Pay particular attention to the valves; they're more prone to leakage than the rest of the system.

Check the crawlspace (if you have one) to make sure that the plumbing lines are insulated. Unless you live in the Sunbelt and never have freezing conditions, insulating the lines in a ventilated crawlspace will reduce energy costs, and will prevent frozen pipes and the nightmare that a major flood presents. In the State of Washington, this is a mandatory identification baked into our Standard. Check with your own state to see if they have similar requirements.

Functional Flow

One test that the inspector will run is a functional flow test in which he/she will turn the water on at multiple fixtures to test the flows.

Older galvanized plumbing, for example, may have a very substantial pressure drop when more than one or two fixtures operate at the same time or when the toilet gets flushed. Galvanized material deteriorates from the inside out causing the interior diameter to become constricted. Unfortunately, reduced flow is a warning sign that a potentially large repair is on the horizon. More often, the issue is undersized piping leading to the fixtures. There simply is very little that you can do about this except to disclose it.

Remember earlier when I suggested that maybe you don't want a pre-listing inspection? This is why... however, there is a very real chance that the next inspector will find it anyway. Since you aren't trained to judge the signs yourself, any test you do on functional flow is purely informational. The inspection may identify a drop, but unless the loss of flow is severe, most sellers don't upgrade the supply plumbing.

Water Pressure

Related to functional flow, but not the same, is water pressure. When I first bought my current home, the water came out of the showerhead like a fire hose tackling a four-alarm torch job. Unfortunately, no matter how popular the fire hose effect is for my daughters trying to rinse soap out of their hair, it's not good for the plumbing system.

The plumbing is a highly engineered system, as are all of the fittings, fixtures, and appliances attached to the supply plumbing. High water pressure can cause early degradation of the appliances. Dish and clothes washers are designed to operate at specific pressures, usually 15 to 80 PSI. Increasing these also increases the wear and tear on the equipment, shortening their service lives.

Ideally, you would like to see the water pressure between 40 and 80 PSI (Pounds per Square Inch) when you test it. If you do measure and discover that you have high water pressure, correction of the problem is as simple as installing a Pressure Reducing Valve near the main valve where the primary water supply enters the building.

Now, I did say "as simple as" but that doesn't mean that I recommend that you do it yourself. This work should be done by a licensed plumber, especially in older homes that may have degrading supply lines. It is not an expensive repair and I feel it is worth having a person with the training and proper tools to tackle a job that, done incorrectly, would have a geyser spraying across the house. Just something to think about.

Plumbing Checklist

- ✓ Verify that the hot and cold water are on the correct sides. Cold on the right, hot on the left.
- ✓ Make sure all the stoppers work.
- ✓ Test all the sinks for leaks.
- ✓ Does the water drain quickly? If not, clear the clogs.
- ✓ Look for leaks on the supply piping. Pay attention to joints and valves. Repair any that appear suspicious.
- ✓ Turn on both hot and cold water at the tub and the sink. Turn on the kitchen faucet. Flush the toilet. There might be a slight drop – that's okay. If any fixture drops by 50 percent, call a plumber.
- ✓ If you want to test water pressure, buy a gauge. Attach it to the cold water bib for the washer (put a bucket below to catch drips), and turn on the bib. The pressure should be 40-80 PSI. If higher or lower, contact a plumber. If you have a pressure reducer already installed, adjust yourself.

Chapter 7 – Heating and Cooling

This section will be short. Most homeowners are not trained HVAC (Heating, Ventilation, and Air Conditioning) technicians and I am assuming you are in this larger group. I strongly recommend retaining the services of a qualified HVAC contractor.

Service your equipment!

Get the furnace and air conditioner serviced as close to the day you list the property as possible. Your Realtor may wish to see this done earlier but I suggest waiting so that the date on the service sticker tag will be more recent. If you think that you are at least a year away from listing, do it now and repeat it in one calendar year.

The home inspector will be looking for the service tag for two reasons. The first is the obvious one, to find out if a HVAC (Heating, Ventilation, Air Conditioning) technician recently inspected the equipment and serviced it. However, the technicians in our area are notorious for not putting tags on the equipment or failing to update the existing tag. If I don't see an updated tag or indicator that the equipment has been serviced, my comment on servicing will read:

> *The furnace does not appear to have been recently serviced (no service sticker was observed/not current). Safe@Home Inspections recommends that furnace cleaning, service and certification be performed by a qualified contractor, with measurements according to the data plate. If the current owner has had the unit serviced but the servicing company did not put on a sticker, he/she should have records and receipts that could be accepted in lieu of the new service.*

Older Equipment

Older gas- or oil-fired furnaces or boilers (anything older than ten years old if an ultra-high efficiency furnace or boiler, older than fifteen years for all others) should have the heat exchanger checked for cracks and leaks.

Save your receipts

Save all your work orders, receipts, and manuals in one location. We'll talk about what to do with these later. For now, if you can, ask the service technician to make sure that they notate the purpose of the visit on the existing tag or to put on a new tag.

Air conditioners

Outside

Check around the outside of the air conditioner (the condenser component) to make sure that the fins are clean of debris and that there is proper air flow around the unit. This may mean trimming back vegetation. Check the condition of the insulation on the line sets – the copper tubing that extends from the unit to the evaporator inside the home. Insulation should be on the thicker suction line but not on the skinnier liquid line. It's a fast and inexpensive fix to put more insulation around it so be sure to repair this if needed.

If the inspection is taking place in winter and you typically cover the condenser with a tarp or other protective material, remove it just for the day of the inspection. Even if the inspector cannot test the air conditioner because temperatures are too cold for safe operation, he can visually assess the unit and share basic information regarding age and size, as well as the apparent general condition.

Inside

The evaporator unit should have been recently serviced and the interior cleaned. If you have signs of leakage, mention it to the service technician and ask that he notate on the service sticker that it was addressed – preferably with wording that indicates that no on-going issue was observed.

Make sure the condensate is headed either to the exterior of the home or to a drain. It may do this by means of a condensate pump or by a gravity feed pipe. If the discharge is to a floor drain, ensure that the water drops cleanly into the drain and that there is nothing blocking the drain or the pipe. I've seen blockages occur due to algae growth at the pipe opening causing the water to back up all the way into the furnace impeller motor casing. It took two seconds to clear the pipe and get the water flowing again.

Wall-Mounted Air Conditioners

Clean the filters and dust the exterior casing. If the outside wall where the air conditioner pokes out is not sealed, I suggest doing it to keep cool air in and bugs out.

Window Air Conditioners

Window air conditioners are outside the scope of inspection. If you have one installed, make it look clean and professional, with appropriate bracing so it's not leaning or tipping in or out of the window.

Central Air Handlers

Filters

Take advantage of another opportunity to build a good impression by changing your filter monthly during the time that the home is listed. A dirty filter grosses people out. Filters are cheap. Don't let this small step get in your way!

Ducts

Many homebuyers are worried about mold and indoor allergens. Because of this, these buyers tend to gravitate toward the duct systems and will be looking inside the diffusers (the floor vents) for dust and detritus. If they see two-year-old Cheerios turning green in there, you can expect a negative response. You may not (and probably do not) need to do a full duct cleaning, which can easily cost hundreds of dollars. I do suggest vacuuming the bottom of the floor vents to the first curve in the duct. Remove the diffusers and use the extension on you vacuum cleaner to poke inside the opening and remove all the loose materials.

If any of the diffusers are broken or show excessive wear-and-tear, replace them.

On the day of the inspection, make sure that all of the diffusers are in the open position. This makes it easier for the inspector to determine if there is airflow into the room.

On a related note, if you have heavy furniture parked on top of a vent, think about moving it. Otherwise, the inspector may leave this as an open question to be answered later, either on an expensive return visit or on an additional service call.

Thermostats

Thermostats should be clearly visible – please don't hide them behind pictures or under a tall fern. Most modern thermostats have a battery backup and some won't work with dead batteries. Check the batteries and swap for new ones if the little indicator on the screen is blinking at you.

If you have a new-fangled high tech thermostat that does fancy things like interact with the utility via the Internet, please leave me a note and a manual. I absolutely guarantee that I will play with that thing until I figure out how it works – but it will put me behind schedule and, when I try to explain the unit's operation to the buyer, I will likely engender some confusion.

Alternate Heating Sources

Baseboard Heat

If you have a house that has baseboard or in-wall electric, make sure that both the controls and the heating elements are visible and accessible. I strongly recommend removing all combustible materials (like curtains) from in front of the heaters. The inspector will spot the unsafe condition; if he should mention it to the buyer this will introduce doubt into their minds. You don't need that hassle. Be proactive on this, even if it means removing the curtains.

Fireplaces

If you have a wood-burning fireplace, and use it on a regular basis, have it professionally cleaned. Make sure the company hired to clean the chimney is licensed and trained for the work. They should also check the damper function and interior components. If the fireplace has been used as a decorative alcove feature and has not had a fire, you can probably skip this step.

If you haven't used the fireplace because a previous inspection determined it was not safe to operate, disclose this.

Gas stove manufacturers recommend annual service of the gas log fireplace by trained professionals. You should clean and maintain the burner components and do a routine inspection of the vents yourself. If you do hire a pro, they will check the fuel/air mixture to make sure that the fireplace operates at optimum efficiency, check for gas leaks, and inspect the blower components to ensure the fan operates correctly.

Access

On the day of the inspection double-check that the areas in front of all the mechanical equipment – furnace, air conditioner, water heater, fireplace – are clear of any obstacles. Make sure there is at least 36 inches of space in front and to the sides. Inspectors need room to remove the covers, inspect the interiors of the cabinets, and to stand.

HVAC Checklist

- ✓ Service the furnace and air conditioner. Request the technician mark the service tag with the date.
- ✓ Change the filter.
- ✓ Uncover the condenser if you have it protected against winter weather.
- ✓ Clear vegetation around the condenser to ensure proper air flow.
- ✓ Check the insulation on the refrigerant lines. Replace if damaged.
- ✓ Check to make sure the condensate lines are draining correctly.
- ✓ Check the ductwork at the diffusers. Decide if they are okay, need to be vacuumed, or due for professional duct cleaning.
- ✓ Check the thermostat for function. It should be secure to the wall with all pieces intact. Replace batteries if necessary.
- ✓ Leave directions for use if the thermostat is a fancy high-tech system integrated into your smart phone. The inspector will thank you for this!
- ✓ If you use your fireplace on a regular basis, get a chimney sweep out to clean and inspect it. Test the damper yourself to make sure it works smoothly.
- ✓ Consider servicing gas fireplaces to manufacturer's recommendations.
- ✓ Remove combustibles (rags, paint cans, boxes) from in front of gas/oil-fired furnaces or water heaters. Make sure power cords and curtains do not drape over electric heaters.

Chapter 8 – Crawlspaces

What kind of foundation do you have? There are three fundamental styles of foundation construction in the United States: slab-on-grade construction, foundation wall with footings (basements or crawlspaces), and post and beam. Each will have different issues that you need to be aware of prior to the inspector arriving on your doorstep.

Remember, we're not interested in doing major renovation work. If you have a failing foundation wall or broken post-tension reinforcement, you are well beyond the DIY limit and need to hire a quality contractor or engineer to get the problem fixed.

For our purposes, I am going to focus on crawlspaces. The only functional difference between a basement and a crawlspace is the height of the area below your floor. In most cases, a crawlspace will have a soil floor rather than finished concrete. In both cases, you have a footing supporting a foundation wall, usually with interior supports to hold up the floor joists. Several elements are applicable to basements as well, especially when we discuss water intrusion.

If you do nothing else... Make the crawlspace accessible.

By that, I literally mean make the hatch accessible. Since most people aren't using their crawlspaces on the daily basis, it's common for the access hatches to be completely covered by, well, stuff! Remove the collapsible shoe rack, or the bike helmets and fourteen soccer balls, the boxes, vacuums, and storage units, the litter boxes, boxes of books, the complete set of weights for a body builder, tools, Christmas decorations, guns, ammunition, carboys of beer brewing (really!), and the four thousand other items that I have seen stacked right on top of the access. It all has to go somewhere else.

Sorry if I sound cranky but this is a major peeve of inspectors. Many will not move personal belongings and so the space will be noted as uninspected with a recommendation for follow-up. Dire warnings on the importance of inspecting this area will be conveyed to the buyer. This is not good for you!

You want the inspector in the crawlspace. He wants to be in there (well, he *should*, at least!). Please make it easier for him to do his job. Clear everything off the access. If it is under carpet, roll the carpet back. If it's on the exterior and locked, remove the lock.

What to prep for a crawlspace

The general rule for crawlspaces is that they should be at least 18 inches deep, measured from the bottom of your floor joists, and 12 inches from the beams. Older houses often will not have the proper clearances and the inspector will almost certainly note it along with a recommendation to dig it out to the proper depths. This is not easily correctable, but you want to be aware of it. I don't recommend taking action on it unless your deal hinges on it.

It may seem obvious but the area should be dry. If there is standing water, the source needs to be identified and corrected. Always report a known water intrusion. Sometimes the water is from wind-driven rain coming through a vent. If so, it should be a very small amount and located near the windward vents. Most real estate forms will ask about it—be proactive, identify the type of intrusion, and the action taken to relieve the issue. Build confidence in your competence. Letting the inspector discover an intrusion event will generate anxiety in the buyer.

Vapor Barriers

A vapor barrier is a 6-millimeter thick black plastic sheet that is laid on the ground to prevent the release of water vapor from the ground into the space. The average crawlspace is capable of releasing gallons of water to atmosphere. This water can condense on the wood and concrete surfaces and cause mold, wood rot or encourage pest infestations (termites and wood destroying beetles). What you want see is a plastic moisture barrier across the entire area with any seams taped. The plastic should extend over the base of the footing (if visible) and about 6 inches up the wall.

If you don't have any plastic down, I strongly recommend installing it, since it is a requirement for FHA, VA and USDA loans. If you have a barrier but it doesn't cover all the soil, add more plastic as needed to provide coverage.

Venting

The crawlspace is normally vented to remove water vapor from the confined space. More modern houses may have a conditioned crawlspace, which is designed without the traditional vents. In the case that you do have vents, be sure that they are covered with a wire mesh screen to prevent pest entry. Every inspector has stories of finding a cat or rabbit, long deceased, in the crawlspace. Buyers don't like dead things in their home, so preventing entry is important. If you do have dead things, remove them.

Foundation Walls

The walls around the perimeter will be made of concrete, masonry block, stone, or wood. They should be free of major cracks (some hairline cracking in concrete is typical).

The wood should be in good condition, without any signs of mold or rot. Pay particular attention to the corners, as these are common areas for wood rot and termite trouble. To test for rot, use a screwdriver or awl to poke into the wood. Sound wood will not give way. Also, make a note of any wood that is in contact with the ground. Earth-to-wood contact will be reported and may affect financing.

Cleaning

Finally, if there are boxes, fallen insulation, scrap wood, etc. in the crawlspace, remove them. All of these items encourage pest intrusion and make it very challenging for the inspector to give an accurate opinion of the space.

Crawlspace Checklist

- ✓ Make it accessible.

- ✓ Make sure there is a vapor barrier and that it is intact.

- ✓ Make sure the crawlspace is dry. If not, the source of water needs to be located and corrected.

- ✓ Check the vents. Screens should be intact.

- ✓ Do a sweep of the perimeter of the foundation. If you have a very large crack, call a specialist.

- ✓ Look at the wood – is any of it obviously rotted, or significantly discolored? If so, call a specialist.

- ✓ Correct any earth-to-wood conditions.

- ✓ Remove leftover construction materials, insulation, etc. from the space.

Chapter 9 – The Attic

The Washington State Standards of Practice that I operate under requires the inspector to enter and traverse the attic space (provided it is safe to do so). All the Standards require some form of inspection, though not all of them expressly make the inspector enter the attic.

Access

Like the crawlspace, attic hatches can be a bother to get into. This can be the result of poor design during building, commonly seen in houses built before 1970. In other cases, the restricted access is caused by the homeowner.

There is little that I would advise you to do for a hatch that is: A) too small; or, B) awkwardly located. A 1940's home with the hatch in the hall closet that is narrower than my shoulders is not atypical. To try to resize it would not be a reasonable activity at this point when there are many more beneficial projects you might consider.

Some homes have a hatch located in a closet with shelves blocking the opening. Please unload the shelf and remove any objects that block the hatch. If possible, remove a couple of shelves to make it easier to squeeze past. I can fit through a space smaller than my shoulders, but I still need space to maneuver.

Special considerations for accesses in master closets

A large percentage of newly constructed homes in my region are now putting the attic hatch in the master closet. This works very effectively for the size requirements of a modern access. However, this can be a two-fold problem for inspectors. First, sometimes the owner will store boxes, laundry baskets, etc. on the floor under the hatch. Please try to clear this area.

The second problem, at least for me, is that I am almost certain to cause a small amount of insulation to fall from the hatch on opening. Your clothes are directly below. I do my best to avoid getting the fiberglass or cellulose on your possessions but I could use help. Take a moment to cover your clothes with a bed sheet to protect them. If you have nicer clothes that say "dry-clean only," please remove them and set them across your bed where they will stay undisturbed.

Special considerations for accesses in garages

Garages are interesting rooms. My rough estimate is that a full fifty percent of garages are never used to park a vehicle. While using this space for extra storage is understandable, it does pose a problem for an inspector who needs to set up a ladder. Before the day of inspection, clear some floor space for the legs of the ladder with ample room on either side for the inspector to set up and take down the ladder.

If your car is in the garage, it needs to move, especially if it usually sits under the hatch. If the car is there and in the way, the inspector will call the attic as inaccessible. None of us are willing to risk dropping something on that car. For the period of the inspection, please put your personal or classic auto in a place other than under the hatch.

Special considerations for accesses in knee walls

A knee wall is a short wall that is used to support the rafters and is usually seen in older homes on either side of a finished attic. Since it is a wall, things tend to get stacked in front of this type of access. Please move items so that the access is both visible and accessible to the inspector.

What if there is no access?

Certain styles of construction do not have attics or accesses. These include flat-roof homes, manufactured homes, and homes with Structurally Insulated Panels (SIPs). This is nothing to fret about as it is typical of the style.

If you do have a full attic but no access, consider putting one in as it should be called by the buyer's inspector and will end up on the addendum later. I recommend a contractor for this project.

What if the hatch cover is sealed with caulk?

I don't know how common this is in other parts of the country, but in my corner of Washington State, the attic hatches are sometimes sealed to limit air intrusion/heat loss. Before I cut that caulk, I always get permission. Speed up the process by either cutting the caulk yourself or leaving written permission in a note.

What to look for in the attic

You should not plan on doing extensive work in the attic but I want you to look for a few hot-button issues. NOTE: Unless you are trained for movement in the dark, in confined spaces, and are part monkey, I do not recommend you traverse the attic. Do your observations from the hatch. Most inspectors will also inspect from the hatch, especially if they judge the attic to be hazardous to enter due to low clearances or there is a potential of hidden wiring and piping that can be damaged by an inadvertent step.

Insulation

You have to have at least some insulation in your attic. This sounds flippant but you'd be shocked at how many attics don't have insulation at all, or just a couple of inches. This is a relatively inexpensive fix and will start paying you back immediately in lower utility costs. Adding insulation in the average attic is within Easy DIY levels if you're able to enter your attic safely and feel comfortable in that environment. Also, check the local utilities for rebates. Many have a rebate program that will partially offset the cost of insulating.

Framing

While you are at the attic hatch, look for any signs of broken wood —rafters or trusses—that should be addressed. These are usually less expensive to repair than you might guess. Broken wood is also less common than you might expect, despite any horror stories you may have heard.

A more common framing issue is that the entire roof structure is old and was not built to the current standard. Unless the materials show an indication of failure, most inspectors will note it but not recommend unreasonable upgrading. If they do, your Realtor will go to bat for you.

Mold

While you're looking around your attic, look for evidence of mold. This is a "must-do" and the reason is simple: It will cause you untold headaches if you don't address a mold issue prior to the inspection.

Now, before you get too excited, first look and see if the plywood, wood, or OSB (a kind of manufactured structural panel) is in good shape. The surface should be relatively clean though you may see signs of discoloration from aging and heat. These are different from mold and are usually uniform across the attic space. If everything looks to be in pristine condition, celebrate.

Spots or splotchy areas, on the other hand, could be mold. But...

Don't Panic!

That reaction you're having? That's what the buyers will go through, too. So, this is something that needs to be addressed, but rationally.

First, evaluate the extent of the issue. Is it localized? If so, recognize that the EPA and most state agencies do not recommend testing – they recommend *addressing* the problem. In this case that means locating the source of moisture that's promoting mold growth, removing that source, and drying the affected materials thoroughly. Oftentimes, cleaning is not even required though I recommend that you consider it.

Again, don't panic! This is nothing unmanageable. The simple fact is that not all molds are toxic (in fact, very few are) and the physics of home design and operation make attic mold less likely to enter the living spaces.

I'm going to quote the EPA (Environmental Protection Agency):

> *Fix plumbing leaks and other water problems as soon as possible. Dry all items completely.*
>
> *Scrub mold off hard surfaces with detergent and water, and dry completely...*
>
> *Do not paint or caulk moldy surfaces. Clean up the mold and dry the surfaces before painting. Paint applied over moldy surfaces is likely to peel.*

The mandatory step here is to control that moisture. That will fundamentally limit the growth of the fungus. There are two reasons to consider the last step, painting. First, it blocks the potential release of spores by encapsulating them. Second, it acts as a warning system in the event of re-growth.

What if all the sheathing is black?

Don't panic. I know, I said that already, twice, but if the whole attic is looking grim, it bears repeating. Breathe.

For an extensive issue, it's time to call in professionals. Please vet them very carefully. Interview as many as you can before you decide to retain a particular company's services. Be on guard for contractors whose goal is to scare the bejeezers out of you – along with a good chunk of your money. Any remediation company should be fully licensed, certified, and insured.

One item to insist on is a guarantee. A reputable company should be able to remediate the problem and issue a warranty. Such warranties are available. Make sure that it is transferrable to the new owners.

I won't promise that this fix is inexpensive, but it is necessary.

Attic Checklist

✓ Make it accessible.

✓ If the access point is in a closet, help the inspector protect your belongings by removing them before the inspection.

✓ If the access is sealed shut, please cut it before the inspector gets there. You may also leave a note with permission for him to do so. He may or may not, depending on his comfort level (this is well beyond the standards) and his insurance.

✓ Check the framing wood for obviously broken pieces.

✓ If you see what you believe to be fungal growth – mold, mildew, or the equivalent – follow the EPA guidelines for correct. Have a contractor help with the ventilation issues that are a major source of the issue.

✓ Check your insulation. Approximately how deep is it? Decide if you should add insulation. (If you are more than six months away from moving, you will likely see some benefit from adding insulation at the beginning of the home sale process.)

Chapter 10 – Environmental Conditions

Time to touch on a few items that are well outside the normal scope of a home inspection. If you read an Inspection Agreement, you will note that there are a list of items specifically excluded. A Washington State contract, by way of example, states that an inspection does not include investigation of mold, asbestos, lead paint, water, soil, air quality or other environmental issues unless agreed to in writing in the pre-inspection agreement. Most contracts will have these types of exclusions.

Still, some of this may come up at the time of inspection. I will not be covering all the possibilities, but discussing to the more common ones that you might encounter.

Termites/Wood Destroying Organisms

Most states have some degree of pests that will gnaw on your house so you should expect to have a specialty inspection done. If you are selling a home in California, this specialty inspection is automatic and is the responsibility of the seller. Here in Washington State, a wood-destroying organisms inspection is strongly recommended for the west side of the state but, since it's not a requirement, the buyer usually bears the cost. California places the responsibility on the seller. You should check with Realtor to determine the most common practice in your region.

Even without this special inspection, the inspector may find evidence of a pest intrusion and recommend further inspections to assess the scope of the problem and any necessary repairs. Each state has specific laws pertaining to disclosure of events such as termite intrusion. Check with your Realtor for more information.

Some loans, the VA loans in particular, also require special pest inspections to be reported on National Pest Management Association (NPMA) Form 33. The seller is expected to bear the cost. Make sure that the NPMA is sufficient in your state. Washington State requires considerably more information in their reports and does not recognize the

NMPA Form 33 as acceptable. I usually do the NPMA and reference the state-compliant report as an addendum.

If you have previous evidence of an intrusion, get a complete pest inspection done and, for goodness sake, disclose. The buyer's inspector will see the remaining evidence and will report it along with a recommendation for further evaluation by a pest control operator. This is unbelievably scary to the buyers. Be proactive.

Septic Systems

Plan on having the septic system inspected and the tank pumped unless you've done both recently. In which case, keep your receipt and any service notes handy.

Radon

Considered the second leading cause of lung cancer in the United States, radon is an odorless, tasteless, colorless naturally occurring gas. The EPA maintains a map of radon zones, with Zone 1 the most likely to have high radon levels, but they recommend every home be tested. In high radon areas, these tests are nearly automatic and many of the homes have already had mitigation systems installed.

Buyers may ask for this test even in lower risk zones. I have had positive tests in all three zones. Confounding the issue, radon fluctuates from home to home. Houses next door to each other often test with wildly different results.

I do not recommend radon testing for sellers. A positive result can stigmatize the house. Let the buyer decide their level of comfort with or without the testing.

Underground Oil Storage Tanks

If you have an underground storage tank (UST) and it is still in use, have it tested. Tanks can corrode over time and release heating oil into the soil, possibly contaminating water tables. The buyers will want assurances that the tank is intact. When you have it tested, have the system serviced at the same time. Many states have insurance programs set up for USTs. If your state does, consider insuring it. Not all the state insurances are transferrable, so investigate the rules in your state.

If the tank is no longer in service and it has not been decommissioned, I recommend you do so. There is a mistaken fear that doing anything with the tank will trigger EPA requirements for excavation, soil mitigation, and backfill. While it is true that the EPA has regulations in place governing USTs, those regulations apply specifically to tanks with capacities greater than 1,100 gallons. Home heating oil tanks are usually in the 250 to 500 gallons range. The EPA has provided a helpful flowchart to determine if your tank is exempted from their regulations. (Visit www.epa.gov/oust/compend/adn10.pdf)

However, this does not exempt you from state and local regulations, so check carefully. If you decide to decommission your tank, your local fire marshal can be a great source of information and advice.

Mold

We talked about mold in the section about attics. Let's chat a little more...

First, I am presuming that you do not have massive quantities of mold growing up the basement walls or covering the ceiling. If you do, we're well past the scope of this guide.

Fact: Mold occurs naturally and lives in your house. Most household molds are not harmful. *Gasp!* Of course, no one wants to *see* mold and left untreated it can get out of hand. What we will concern ourselves with is mold that is growing on surfaces. The EPA states bluntly: *"If mold is a problem in your home, clean up the mold and get rid of the excess water or moisture."* Please note that they didn't say test, tear out all the walls, or panic.

Mold is often found in bathrooms as a result of homeowners or tenants failing to use the fan or the fan not working. Your grandmother called this stuff mildew, especially when it's found around the tub and shower. The inspector should be noting all such instances in his/her report so be proactive and take care of this before inspection day.

Mold also frequently develops in basement areas, usually due to poor air movement, the natural dampness of below grade construction, and inattention from the homeowner. How often do you really need to pull out the boxes with the Christmas decorations? Ideally, you want to find and correct this issue before an inspector gets his two cents in because not every inspector will follow EPA guidelines. Some will actively scare the client, especially if they're in the "Mold is Gold" camp. To help get ahead of this, look into the backs of closets and along the base of walls where your possessions were stored for evidence of mold.

There is limited evidence that molds cause negative health effects for normally healthy individuals. Those most affected tend to be individuals with allergies, respiratory conditions, and asthma. Often, you will have a small growth area, such as I described above, without having a single health response.

I do not mean to minimize the issue. If you have mold, you must clean it. It is an emotional trigger for the buyer. Also realize that buyers who have existing health issues will likely seek testing. If an actionable level is found, expect to be asked to remediate. But don't panic—it isn't necessary.

For information on cleaning mold from your home, go to the EPA's online Mold Cleanup Guidelines.

Asbestos

Asbestos is another trigger substance. Commonly used in a wide range of building materials (and still in use in some today that you can buy at the local hardware store,) asbestos was a miracle fiber for decades.

Then the health problem associated with it—mesothelioma, lung cancer, and asbestosis—became known. The risk of developing the diseases is correlated with the levels of exposure. Miners of vermiculite in Libby, MT have had a very high incidence rate of disease.

In your home the risk is less, but present.

Asbestos is not identifiable in the field and requires a laboratory to perform the proper testing, so an inspector is not going to be able to positively identify harmful materials. Nor may the inspector test for asbestos in many states unless they have the requisite training and certifications.

The EPA recommends that the safest practice is to leave undamaged materials alone. Indeed, the simple act of testing it can make the material more hazardous (the EPA recommends against you doing this yourself.)

If the material is damaged, you should seek the assistance of professionals trained to work with the material. They will evaluate your circumstances and make the decision to remove, encapsulate, or seal depending on the type of material and the severity of the damage.

More information regarding asbestos is readily available at the EPA's radon website and click "Protect Your Family."

Environmental Conditions Checklist

Pests/Termites

✓ Determine if your state requires sellers to provide this inspection.

✓ If you live in a region noted for pests, be proactive and do this immediately before listing your home.

✓ If you live in a region with a significant military population likely to use VA loans, be proactive and do this immediately before listing your home.

Septic Systems

✓ Schedule a septic inspection immediately before listing the property. It is a given that the buyer will request this.

Radon

✓ What is the local convention in your area? If radon monitoring is routine, get it out of the way.

✓ If you have a mitigation system that is more than 2 years old, it is time to perform follow up monitoring.

✓ If rarely asked for in your region, wait for the buyer to make the request.

Underground Oil Storage Tanks

✓ Is a tank present? If so, do you have documentation that decommissioning has taken place in accordance with local ordinances? If not, begin the process, following all the applicable regulations.

Mold

✓ Determine if you have a mold/mildew issue.

✓ Does it appear to be a surface condition in the bathroom? If so, improve ventilation, clean thoroughly in accordance to EPA guidelines.

Can you determine the source of the water that is allowing for growth? Check for proper ventilation in attics and crawlspaces. Look for leaks in under-cabinet spaces. Look for leaks around windows, doors, and the roof.

✓ If you cannot identify the water source, call an expert with the appropriate tools.

✓ Do you have an event in the attic or crawlspace that *you* feel is severe? If you even hesitate to answer that question, bring in a Certified Mold Assessor. Science will not trump emotion, but it helps. Get facts and take the appropriate action

Asbestos

✓ Was your home built before 1980? If yes, there is a chance you have some asbestos present. Check to see if the local regulations are more strict than EPA guidelines.

✓ Check for: 9x9 flooring tiles, popcorn ceilings, white pipe wrap on radiator or hot water lines, cement fiber shingles on the exterior of the home, white rigid board backing furnaces, or vermiculite in the attic.

✓ If you have any of the above, are the components intact? If so, stop now. Remediation often makes the problem worse, not better.

✓ If the material is in poor repair with loose pieces, call a specialist for remediation. Beware of someone who tells you it all **must** be removed. Sealing or covering is recommended by the EPA for minor repairs. Removal is usually only done on a major remodel.

Chapter 11 – The Inspection is Imminent

It's time to wrap this up. We've covered a lot of ground but now you have received an offer, accepted it contingent to inspection, and the appointment with the inspector is just days away. If you started on this process when you first listed your home, much of this information will be repetitive. That's okay; just go down the checklists at the end to make sure that you have everything ready. Then, celebrate because you've handled this as well as a seller can.

If you jumped right to this chapter because the inspector is standing on your doorstep, it is too late to attempt quality repairs. Instead, I am going to perform triage and tackle absolutely critical items. This chapter will describe what to do for each item on the checklist. Take ten minutes (probably less) and read it.

A word of advice: avoid getting caught short on time by putting these quick tasks on your schedule. Don't leave it to a chance gap in your day as those always fill in. Schedule the walk-around, the shopping, the cleaning, and the light maintenance early.

The Home Manual

Earlier in the book, I suggested saving all your receipts for any work you have completed. Time to get them out. We are going to use a quality three-ring binder (avoid the cheap ones, please!) and put together a "manual" for the home, just like new builders do. You will need dividers, too.

You can start this project prior to the buyer's offer and, if you have good documentation, I suspect your agent will love you for doing this.

Using the dividers, make four sections in the binder.

Section One: Place a copy of the MLS sheet that the real estate agent used for the flyers. Behind this, put in a floor plan of the home. If your home is new enough, you probably still have the one from your builder. If not, make your own using the computer or graph paper. The dimensions do not need to be perfect. The goal is to provide the buyer with an overview of the layout. Mark the following on the floor plan:

- Water Main
- Electrical panels
- Alarm system controls
- Sprinkler Controls
- Crawlspace Access
- Attic Access

That is all you need. Avoid the temptation to indicate every single door, window, electrical receptacle and switch. Do not label the rooms. What you consider a bedroom may be a den to the buyer.

After the floor plan, put in copies of any plat maps you have as well as the legal description of the property. You can get these from your agent (if she hasn't already put it together for you in the sales materials).

If you prepared this ahead of time, have spare sets of this section that potential buyers can take with them. The same goes for the following section.

Section Two: Put copies of your utility bills for the preceding twelve months as well as tax records.

Section Three: Add copies of all the receipts you can find. At a minimum, have the service receipts for the HVAC equipment. If you had any other work done by a handyman, general contractor, painter, they should be included here, too.

Section Four: Put all the warranties and manuals you have, except for the furnace and water heater (those need to stay with the equipment). All the appliance manuals (refrigerator, oven, washing machine, etc.), roof warranties, siding or paint warranties, and similar materials go into this section.

Section Five (Optional): Include a copy of the pre-listing inspection you did, along with the follow-up report showing which repairs have been made. You can also leave this as a separate folder.

Building the Shopping list:

Take notes while you do all of the following checks so you can make a fast to-do and shopping list:

- Go through every room in the house. Check each light bulb to ensure that it works. If you notice a few bulbs burned out, add them to your list.

- Check each room for a smoke detector. If you can't remember when the batteries were last changed, do so now.

- If you have a solid-fuel appliance, gas-fired equipment, or an attached garage, check for carbon monoxide with a carbon monoxide detector.

- Check the filter in the furnace. It should be clean. If it isn't, put the size on the shopping list.

- Check your cleaning supplies. If you are low on anything, restock.

Once you have all the items on the list, take the time to actually install the bulbs, etc. Though it sounds silly, I can't tell you how many times I have made a note of missing detectors or bulbs while the replacements are sitting right there on the kitchen counter. If it isn't installed, it doesn't count.

Maintenance Items:

- Make sure the lawn is mowed and the areas around the base of the walls are clear.

- Check the vegetation for clearance, even if you did it recently. Trim as necessary – you want at least one foot of clearance to the side of the home and ten feet from the roof (if possible.)

- Check the gutters and clean if necessary.

- Make sure all the sidewalks are clear of toys, debris, etc.

- Start the last cleaning of the home. If you don't have time to clean everything, focus on the bathrooms and kitchen.

- Stock the bathrooms with fresh rolls of toilet paper.

- If you have already started packing, put all the boxes into the garage but not against the wall. If you don't have a garage, select one room and stack in the center of the room.

- Check to make sure that most of the electrical receptacles are unobstructed and the heating vents are clear so that the inspector will be able to check both.

- Clear the space in front of the electrical panel. Safety requirements are to have 36 inches in front of the panel and 30 inches to each side. All the screws should be accessible. If a cabinet was built around the panel, remove the cabinet. Do the same with any shelving.

- Remove all personal items from the crawlspace access area. If the scuttle is hidden by carpet, please pull it back.

- The attic hatch should be accessible. Inspectors will need room to set up their ladder, so have at least a three-foot square area cleared below the hatch. If the access is in a closet, remove items from the upper shelves. Opening the hatch almost always creates a drifting storm of falling insulation. If you don't want fiberglass on your clothing, please remove the clothes or place a sheet over the clothing. In some areas, the hatch gets sealed shut with caulk. You'll need to leave written permission for the inspector to cut the opening, or just do it yourself.

- If the house is vacant, either you or your appointed representative should verify that the power and water are turned on, and that all pilots are lit. Breakers should be placed in an "On" position. Refrigerators should be plugged in.

If you stayed organized with all this and planned ahead, the actual effort you need to expend the day of the inspection is minimal. Use the checklist at the end of the chapter to make sure you are on track.

If you didn't plan ahead and the inspector is on his way, go to the checklist. Now. You have some work to do pronto.

Pets:

Please help us keep your four-legged family members comfortable and safe. A home inspection often stresses out even the most mellow of dogs. We need to find a safe location for them. Dogs are territorial to varying degrees and the inspector gets viewed as an intruder, especially if you are stressed, too. We need to provide them with a sense of security. The best option is to remove the animal from the premises. If that is not possible, consider providing them with a comfortable kennel and some water rather than locking them in a room or the garage. Many inspectors will not enter a space with an unfamiliar dog no matter how friendly it seems.

The other concern that inspectors have is accidentally allowing a cherished pet to escape to the great outdoors. Dogs and cats can be astonishingly quick.

Cats can be more difficult. They can be hard to get into kennels, so removing them from the premises is challenging. If the cat is an indoor-only cat, consider sequestering them to a single room and leaving a note for the inspector. This permits the inspector to tackle the cat on his schedule without having to worry about the feline slipping past the inspector's legs and out of the house.

The morning of the inspection, please walk the yard and pick up any piles your dog may have left behind. If you have a cat, change the kitty litter. It's hard to inspect when your eyes are watering from the fumes that a dirty cat box generates.

The Day of the Inspection:

Your Realtor notified you as to the time of the inspection but you should expect the inspector to be a bit early. Most of us hate to be late and arriving early gives us a few precious minutes to get our tools and ladders from our vehicle. I usually try to be five to ten minutes early but some inspectors will aim for a half-hour.

If this creates issues for you, let your Realtor know ahead of time. I have rearranged schedules to accommodate sellers who have set nap times for children or a hectic morning routine. Please be considerate of the buyer and inspector though—I had a seller who so sharply defined the times that she would permit an inspection that I finally asked the agent if she was serious about selling the house. The buyer was feeling a similar frustration. Fortunately the agents finally found a way for us to work together to complete the inspection and kept everything moving forward.

You also need to decide if you wish to meet the inspector. If you choose to, maintain a friendly, professional demeanor. As a visitor in your home, a brief tour pointing out the locations of the accesses, water mains, panels, and such is helpful.

If you don't wish to meet him or her, leave a note covering the same information if the locations are not obvious (water mains come to mind, as these get squirreled behind panels in odd locations).

I also recommend leaving a short note to the buyers. As a home inspector, I rarely get uncomfortable in someone else's home. Most buyers will feel, with some justification, that they are intruding. Aim for simplicity:

> Hi,
>
> Thank you for visiting our home. Please take your time with the inspector – we want you to be as happy in this home as our family has been. Feel free to explore closets, cabinets, and cupboards – we understand.
>
> If you or the inspector have any questions during the inspection, I can be reached at 208-xxx-xxxx.
>
> Thanks again!

Occasionally, sellers will leave out snacks or treats. I don't recommend it as a number of people have allergies that in some cases can be quite severe. I do suggest leaving out bottled water or clean glasses for water. Leave a note to let them know that you want them to use the glasses or they will be reluctant make dirty dishes.

Who Is the Inspector?

Your agent will have informed you of who the inspector is. You need to know more than the name, however. The following is the minimum information that you should acquire about the person entering your home.

First, he should be professionally licensed, if the state requires it. He should have a business license if required (and most municipalities do require it).

He should carry General Liability insurance on the very rare chance that he breaks something. Those are the minimums to keep your possessions and home protected.

What if I Can't Leave?

First, breathe. It happens that sometimes you can't leave. If that is the case, make sure everyone knows ahead of time. Surprises are never good in the inspector universe.

My suggestion is to pick a room that you will be comfortable in. Ask the inspector to finish that room first so you can retreat to it in full privacy. This also allows the buyer (if present) and inspector to communicate without worrying that you will be overhearing their commentary. Remember that their discussion counts as private and privileged in a business sense—and perhaps in legal sense as well, depending on the state.

After the Inspection

The most important action you can take post-inspection is to do nothing. You will be itching to get the report and the buyer's addendum (or, ideally, a signature releasing the contingency).

The buyer and the buyer's agent will not be feeling the same urgency. Most Realtors advise their clients to take a few days and think over the report's findings. This allows them time to discharge the emotional energy the buyer had invested in the inspection.

When you do receive the report, scan it for the major items that the buyer is requesting. If you've prepared well, that list should be very manageable with zero surprises. If there are major surprises, hold your emotions in check. Under no conditions should you call the inspector to berate them. I can state with rock-solid assurance that the inspector will discount everything you say if the first words out of your mouth are something to the effect of, "You're an idiot" or "You scare people by . . ."

Instead, if you have questions request clarifications on the nature of the issue and why the inspector made the decision to mark it as he did. As an inspector, I generally prefer to discuss these with the agents involved, provided I have the approval of my clients. Oftentimes, a bit of conversation can add a great deal of clarity to the situation.

The Inspector Left My Home a Mess

This should never happen but I do hear stories of inspectors who did not show any respect for the home or the owners. In one especially egregious case, the inspector stepped in dog poo in the yard and then wandered all over the house. He was of the opinion that the owner was at fault for not cleaning the yard. He absolutely should have paid for carpet cleaning but did not.

If you have a problem with the way the inspector left your home from a cleanliness standpoint, tell your agent. Word gets around the real estate community quickly and the inspector will shape up or be out of business in short order.

The inspector is morally obligated to leave your home in nearly the same condition as he found it. If something gets damaged, the inspector should leave you a note. If he or she does not, contact your Realtor immediately. Take pictures of the damage before you disturb anything. Send these to your Realtor. Most inspectors will make amends for mishaps.

"The Inspection is Today!" Checklist

- ✓ Prioritize – Family & Pets first, Access second, Cleaning last. Skip steps that don't fit your needs this morning.

- ✓ Organize (as much as possible) the family and get them ready. Confirm plans for the pets.

- ✓ Print out the *Letter to the Inspector*. Fill in blanks. Leave keys for out-buildings.

- ✓ Leave a note for the buyers.

- ✓ Verify that the furnace, water heater, electrical panel, crawlspace, and attic are accessible. If not, please make them so.

- ✓ Put the morning/lunch dishes into the dishwasher. The sink should be empty.

- ✓ Give the kitchen counters a fast wipe if needed.

- ✓ If you created the Home Manual, place it on the kitchen counter or dining room table. Put the garage door opener next to it.

- ✓ Check the bathrooms. Hang any towels that may be down and flush the toilets.

- ✓ Turn on all lights.

- ✓ Open all the bedroom and bathroom doors.

- ✓ If kenneling the pets, leave a note for the inspector on the door. If the cats are loose, let him/her know if they are allowed outside.

- ✓ Do a fast hike of the yard to clean up after the dog. Clean the litter box.

- ✓ Lock the doors behind you.

- ✓ Breathe. It's going to be fine.

About by Paul Duffau:

Based in Washington State, Paul Duffau's professional accomplishments include winning numerous awards in his inspection service, an appointment to the Washington State Home Inspector Advisory Licensing Board by Governor Gregoire in 2010, and an appointment to the State Building Code Council by Governor Inslee in 2013.

He actively manages a thriving commercial and residential inspection service based in Washington State.

Paul is also author of two novels about women's running, the first of which received national attention for it's "inspiring race scenes." A part-time junior high cross country coach and an ultrarunner, Paul runs the pristine trails in Eastern Washington when not inspecting or writing.

Also by Paul Duffau:

Finishing Kick

Trail of Second Chances

WITHDRAWN

CPSIA information can be obtained
at www.ICGtesting.com
Printed in the USA
LVOW07s1313290717
543051LV00005B/233/P